The Encyclopedia of

Saints

Published by Longmeadow Press
201 High Ridge Road, Stamford, CT 06904

Copyright © 1996
Regency House Publishing Limited
ISBN 0-681-21532-1

© Howard Loxton 1996
The right of Howard Loxton to be identified as the
author of this work has been asserted by him in
accordance with the Copyright, Design and Patents
Act 1988.

Cover and interior design by Annabel Trodd

ISBN 0-681-21539-9

Printed in China

First Longmeadow Press Edition

0987654321

RIGHT: St Antony of Padua *by Domenikos Theotokopoulos (El Greco), (1540-1614).*

OPPOSITE: The altarpiece from the Church of St Zeno in Venice by Andrea Mantegna (1431-1506) shows the Madonna and Child flanked on the left by SS Peter, Paul, John the Evangelist and Zeno and on the right by SS Benedict, Laurence, Gregory and John the Baptist.

FRONT COVER: Saint Cecilia Accompanied by Three Angels *by Michiel I. Coxie (1499-1592).*

BACK COVER: Detail of Saint Cyprian, bishop of Carthage from the Church of Saint Cebria of Cabanyes, early 14th century.

Acknowledgements

Page 2, E.T. Archive/Prado, Madrid; Page 3, E.T.
Archive/Saint Zeno, Verona; Pages 4-5, E.T.
Archive/Prado, Madrid; Page 7, Fine Art Photographic
Library Ltd.; Page 8, Fine Art Photographic Library
Ltd./Private Collection; Page 10, E.T.
Archive/Stadtmuseum, Trier/Salomon Collection; Page
11, Giraudon/The Bridgeman Art Library/ Musée de la
Chartreuse, Douai; Page 12, Giraudon/The Bridgeman Art
Library/The Louvre, Paris; Page 14, The Bridgeman Art
Library/Galleria dell'Accademia, Venice; Page 14, E.T.
Archive/Abbey of Monteoliveto Maggiore, Siena; Page
16, The Bridgeman Art Library/Prado, Madrid; Page 17
top, Lauros-Giraudon/The Bridgeman Art Library/The
Louvre, Paris; Page 17 bottom, E.T. Archive; Page 18 left,

E.T. Archive/National Museum of Sculpture, Valladolid;
Page 20, The Bridgeman Art Library/Kunsthistorisches
Museum, Vienna; Page 21, E.T. Archive/Prado, Madrid;
Page 23, E.T. Archive/San Francesco, Assisi; Pages 24-25,
The Bridgeman Art Library/City of York Art Gallery,
York; Page 26, E.T. Archive/Antalya Museum, Turkey;
Page 27, E.T. Archive/Prado, Madrid; Page 28, Fine Art
Photographic Library Ltd.; Pages 29 and 30, E.T.
Archive/Prado, Madrid; Page 31, E.T. Archive/Saint
Peter's Church, Louvain; Page 33, The Bridgeman Art
Library/Galleria degli Uffizi, Florence; Page 34, E.T.
Archive/San Francesco, Assisi; Page 35, E.T.
Archive/Civic Museum, Udine; Page 37, The Bridgeman
Art Library/ Kunsthistorisches Museum, Vienna; Page 38,
Fine Art Photographic Library Ltd./Private Collection;
Page 40 left, E.T. Archive/Saragoza Museum; Pages 40-
41, The Bridgeman Art Library/The Wallace Collection,

London; Page 42, E.T. Archive/Church of the Gesù,
Rome; Page 44, E.T. Archive/Church of San Isidro
Chinchero, Peru; Page 45, Fine Art Photographic Library
Ltd./Private Collection; Pages 46-47, E.T. Archive/Society
San Giorgio degli Schiavone, Venice; Page 48, Fine Art
Photographic Library Ltd.; Page 49, E.T.
Archive/Memling Museum, Bruges; Page 51, Fine Art
Photographic Library Ltd.; Pages 52-53, The Bridgeman
Art Library/Prado, Madrid; Pages 54-55, The Bridgeman
Art Library/Christie's, London; Page 56, E.T.
Archive/Biblioteca Marciana, Venice; Page 57, E.T.
Archive/Bibliothéque Nationale, Paris; Page 58, E.T.
Archive/National Gallery of Hungarian Art, Budapest;
Page 59, Fine Art Photographic Library Ltd./Private
Collection; Pages 60-61, Giraudon/The Bridgeman Art
Library/ Musée des Beaux Arts, Le Havre; Page 61 right,
The Bridgeman Art Library/Alte Pinokothek, Munich;

Page 63, Fine Art Photographic Library Ltd./Private
Collection; Page 64, Fine Art Photographic Library Ltd.;
Page 65, Don Sutton International Photo Library; Page 67,
The Bridgeman Art Library/Christie's; Page 68, The
Bridgeman Art Library/Courtauld Institute Galleries,
University of London; Page 70, Fine Art Photographic
Library Ltd.; Page 71, E.T. Archive/Metropolitan
Cathedral, Mexico City; Page 72, The Bridgeman Art
Library/The Wallace Collection; Pages 73 and 74 top, Fine
Art Photographic Library Ltd.; Page 74 bottom, E.T.
Archive/National Gallery of Hungarian Art, Budapest;
Page 76, The Bridgeman Art Library/The British Library,
London; Page 77, E.T. Archive/Victoria and Albert
Museum, London; Page 78, The Bridgeman Art
Library/San Lazzaro dei Mendicanti, Venice; Page 79 left,
E.T. Archive/Museum of Santa Cruz, Toledo; Page 79
right, The Bridgeman Art Library/Prado, Madrid.

The Encyclopedia of Saints

Howard Loxton

LP LONGMEADOW PRESS

Introduction

Almost every culture and religion has singled out certain individuals as objects of respect and emulation. These are the people who have led exemplary lives or made some considerable contribution to their society or their religion, or made a particularly striking demonstration of their beliefs. Those who wholeheartedly dedicate their lives to their religion are often seen as holy men and women in their own lifetime and sought out as teachers and counsellors to such an extent that even after their death they, and the places associated with them continue to be the subject of veneration.

Among Hindus, *sadhu* (holy men) or *yogi* (ascetics), both living and dead, are regarded not so much as saints but avatars, or incarnations of a god. To the ancient Greeks, their legendary heroes were given a status halfway between god and man, while Roman emperors were even known to elevate themselves to the status of a god in their own lifetime.

Monotheistic faiths preclude such possibilities, but the idea that particularly holy men and women might have some special intercessionary role in heaven was one which developed early in the Christian Church. This concept was never present in Judaism, though the memory of certain Jewish prophets, patriarchs and martyrs, such as the Maccabees, was sometimes celebrated at their places of burial. Neither was it later accepted by Islam. Although the Prophet Mohammed specifically rejected the idea of saints, the regard in which the common people held certain holy men led to their graves becoming places of pilgrimage and such devotions were thought to aid the believer in acquiring blessings. However, any such blessing or miracles were considered to be the work of Allah alone rather than of these saints, or *wali* as they were known.

To the early Christians a saint could be anyone who was a baptized member of the Church, in much the same way as the confraternity of Christians is still referred to as the 'Communion of Saints' – a phrase specifically employed in the Nicene Creed adopted by the Church in AD 325 – and which is also used by the Mormons to describe the members of their Church of Jesus Christ of Latter-day Saints.

In the centuries when Christians were forced to meet and celebrate their religion in secret, when discovery could bring persecution and even death, those who chose to die rather than renounce their faith were thought to go straight to heaven; it therefore followed that they could be used as intermediaries by the living, being that much closer to God. Martyrs – and it is worth remembering that the original Greek word means 'witness' – were willing to make the supreme sacrifice, the last thing expected of lesser mortals in whom the instinct for self-preservation is at its strongest. It is hardly surprising, therefore, that these exceptional people should be fervently admired and revered given the cruel and often gruesome manner of their deaths. They became the subjects of special veneration and described as saints, attributed with all the characteristics of this special élite as we understand it today. During the 4th century the cult of martyrs was increasingly extended to include virgins and confessors of unique holiness.

At first these cults developed as a localized phenomenon among Christians who had first-hand experience of martyrs and others who appeared to be surrounded by an aura of holiness which manifested itself in their actions. Often, Christians had witnessed miracles attributable to these people in life or at their shrine after death. Sometimes they attracted followers or devotees because of the stories associated with them, because of their connection to a particular trade or profession, or because they were linked to prayers answered and cures performed. Others become known far from their places of origin as missionaries transmitted their devotion to particular saints, spreading knowledge of them to other lands.

Such cults may have sprung up spontaneously around the tomb of a holy person, but public veneration first needed to be approved by the local bishop. A contemporary record of the execution in about AD 155 of Polycarp, bishop of Smyrna, describes how the faithful collected his bones and buried them at a place where they could celebrate each anniversary of his martyrdom. The preservation and veneration of bones and other relics became an important part of the cult of sainthood. It became the custom to

place a relic in a new church and then specifically in an altar at the church's consecration. Relics were, for instance, among the things thought 'necessary for the worship of the Church' which Pope Gregory the Great sent to St Augustine's mission in England. In 787 the Second Council of Nicea ruled that henceforth they were absolutely necessary for the consecration of new churches and that any which had been consecrated without them should acquire some relics as soon as possible.

The possession of a saintly burial, or of important relics, or a catalogue of miracles associated with a particular shrine was a powerful means of attracting pilgrims and benefactions, ensuring that a church or abbey prospered. Places which became the focus of pilgrimage, rather like tourist centres today, could grow rich on the trade they attracted, though popularity could fluctuate according to the frequency of miracles or manner of competition from new cult centres. There was also competition to own relics: sometimes they were seized by raiders and it was not uncommon for more than one church to lay claim to identical parts of a saint's anatomy.

The way in which people came to treat relics and images of the saints bears a striking resemblance to the way their ancestors regarded magic talismans and may have been a way of replacing the local gods of former polytheistic religions. To be worshipped, according to the Church, was the prerogative of God alone, though saints could be venerated; they could be treated as conduits through which prayers could be directed to God though He alone had the power to answer them.

Before a bishop could approve the cult of a saint, certain criteria had to be met. He must be convinced, in the case of a martyr, that he or she had died for love of God and as a witness to the Faith. There must be no question of suicide for reasons of heretical motivation or of acquiring fame. The evidence of miracles was a strong element of proof that a person had been singled out by God. If the bishop was satisfied, the saint's body would be 'elevated' to a shrine for veneration when there could be special celebration on the anniversary of his or her death. Death in this life was recognized as an occasion of rebirth into the next, thus making this date the

most appropriate choice for the festival. Churchmen began to compile hagiographies and martyrologies which helped to spread knowledge of them and saints who were adopted widely found a place in the approved liturgy of the Church with feast days recognized throughout Christendom.

In the Eastern Church, the decision as to whether or not a person should be declared a saint remains to this day with the local bishop. In the West, this rested increasingly with the papacy, probably because, as its power increased, the pope's endorsement carried greater weight so that eventually it became a papal prerogative – though it was not until the early 13th century that it became judicially essential. Papal commissions were now appointed to investigate candidates for sainthood, examining evidence concerning the candidate's life as well as claims of cures and miracles.

In the 16th century the process was assigned to the Congregation of Rites, an office of the papal Curia, and in the following century, any unauthorized public cult was forbidden. The Code of Canon Law,

promulgated in 1917, sets out the procedures by which a person can be added to the list of saints, known as canonization, by the Roman Catholic Church.

The Protestant Churches have no procedures for canonization and have made no new saints since the Reformation. They do not direct their prayers through saints or use them as intermediaries. Denominations differ in the way they view saints but, in general, while they recognize the importance of many individuals in the history of Christianity they do not see them as having a special status in heaven. The Church of England has churches dedicated in the name of many pre-Reformation saints and the liturgical calendar commemorates many of them. Although it does not declare new saints it sets aside particular days to remember individuals whose lives and work have been judged by a Liturgical Commission and the Synod to have contributed to the Universal Church and thus merit commemoration. These are not restricted to members of the Anglican Communion but range ecumenically from Protestant divines to Roman Catholic prelates and a pope.

Lutherans, too, have a calendar which assigns days on which the apostles and early saints can be remembered but Methodists and Baptists, for instance, though they may give an individual the title saint, because to them it is common usage, have no special celebration and use the word only in its general sense of meaning one of God's faithful in heaven, i.e., a member of the Communion of Saints.

The religious conflicts of the Reformation led to persecutions by both sides. While many who died for the Catholic cause during the Reformation or in the missionary field are celebrated as martyrs by the Roman Church, Protestants who suffered equally were, of course, not canonized by their Churches. The Calendar of Saints inevitably includes those who supported orthodoxy to the exclusion of others, not only those who set themselves outside the Catholic Church but those within – a number of saints were churchmen who opposed such movements within the Church as Arianism and Iconoclasm.

The Vatican's 1917 Code recognized two kinds of canonization: formal and extraordinary, the latter a simple papal endorsement of the sainthood of persons whose veneration had already been established for centuries by the time of Pope Urban VIII's reforms in 1634. Formal canonization requires the thorough gathering of evidence on all claims concerning the proposed saint's

holiness or heroic virtue, their writings and the miracles performed by them in life or after death. An advocate or postulator is appointed to present their cause and a promoter of the faith, commonly known as the 'devil's advocate', is appointed to raise objections to the evidence and ensure that the entire truth about the person is made known.

This investigation was once in four stages, the first conducted by the local bishop, three others by the Congregation of Rites and the pope, but in the late 1960s this was modified to make the process shorter and to put the entire process into the hands of diocesan, provincial or regional courts in consultation with the Vatican. Once these processes have been satisfactorily completed, beatification of the candidate is announced at a solemn mass: he or she is declared blessed and veneration approved in specific localities.

For final canonization and declaration as a saint, a similar process is followed. A person who is beatified does not automatically become a saint and, of those who have, it has often taken centuries for papal approval to be given. One essential requirement is that at least two miracles must be authenticated as having taken place since the date of beatification through the invocation of the saint.

In the years leading up to 1969 the Vatican also reviewed the list of saints and the days on which their feasts are celebrated, extending the range of saints worthy of universal veneration and achieving a better balance through countries and centuries, reducing the disproportionate number of saints from certain religious Orders, and in some cases placing an emphasis on local celebration or selecting a more appropriate feast day. It also declared that certain saints of doubtful historical authenticity or for whom there was scanty evidence that they were genuine martyrs should no longer be included in the liturgical Calendar of Saints.

These included several popes and some quite well known names such as Catherine of Alexandria. St Cecilia was retained in the Calendar, possibly because of her enormous popularity and St Christopher and St George were among those reduced to local cult status. Removal from the Calendar does not mean that these saints cannot be venerated, even though we may know nothing certain about them apart from their names.

Over the centuries, the list of saints venerated around the world has come to number many thousands. Even those in the revised Calendar are still far too numerous to include in this volume and new ones are constantly under consideration. The selection of saints that follows must inevitably be a personal one. It is wide ranging and intentionally eclectic, presenting not only saints mentioned in Holy Scripture and other well known names, such as patron saints, but includes some on account of their intriguing stories. There is an acknowledged bias towards saints of interest to the English-speaking world and who have inspired modern Christian names. There is insufficient space to recount all the legends told of many saints and the text concentrates on the most important historical facts of their lives.

The authenticity of many of the early lives of the saints has been questioned, some are clearly inventions, and any modern writer attempting to produce a catalogue must rely heavily upon previous scholarship. This book acknowledges its indebtedness to the many that have gone before. Alban Butler's *Lives of the Saints*, which first appeared in 1756 and is still available in revised editions, was a landmark of hagiography in English, its entries growing in number with the years, while the mammoth *Bibliotheca Sanctorum*, a Latin text in 12 volumes published in Rome in 1960, is probably the most complete even though there have been further canonizations since. For those who require a wider coverage than is

possible here there are several unillustrated dictionaries of saints readily available. They will not agree in every respect either with this book or each other and the reader, too, must feel free to interpret legends, traditions and unauthenticated facts as they feel appropriate.

Religious art has drawn upon legend as much as history in its presentation of saints and at times legend has offered the painter a more attractive facet of the story. Sometimes a genuine portrait has been painted in a saint's own lifetime, and sometimes, especially in the case of the icons of the Orthodox Church, the continuous copying of images by earlier artists has come to establish a standard stylized image. But devotional paintings should not be considered portraiture in the conventional sense. They are there to present a story or encapsulate a spiritual message and this will often be told by means of complex and specific symbolism not always comprehensible to the modern viewer: for instance, when a figure of the infant Jesus is shown sitting on a cloth on his mother's knee it is in fact representing the cloth used in the Eucharist to cover the ciborium and is intended to link the Child Christ with His final sacrifice. Many saints are identified by their different attributes, in the case of Saint Peter, the key or keys indicating that he is the gate-keeper of the Kingdom of Heaven and which were said to have been given to him as Christ's successor on earth. Others are surrounded with the instruments of their martyrdom or objects closely connected with incidents or legends connected with them and well known when the picture was painted. A palm leaf, a pagan symbol of victory, is often carried, especially by martyrs, as a sign of triumph over death, an allusion to a reference in the *Book of Revelations* describing a multitude in heaven standing before the throne of God in white robes and with palms in their hands.

A

Adelaide (931-999) A daughter of a Burgundian king and Empress of the Holy Roman Empire, she was a founder of monasteries and was dedicated to the conversion of the Slavs. At 16 she married the Italian king Lothair who died in 950, probably poisoned by his successor, Berengarius, who imprisoned her when she refused to marry his son. She was freed when the German King Otto invaded, and married him in 951, the year before he became Emperor. After the accession of their son Otto II in 973, conflict with his wife Theophano caused her to leave the court and, though briefly reconciled, she was driven out again when Theophano became regent to his son, Otto III, until on her enemy's death she took over the regency herself. She was buried at Selta, near Cologne, in one of the monasteries she founded. Feast: December 16.

Adrian of Canterbury (d. c.710) An African-born abbot of Nerida near Naples who, though declining the archbishopric of Canterbury, became abbot of the monastery there which was dedicated to SS Peter and Paul (later St Augustine) making it an important seat of learning. Miracles at his tomb added to its fame. Feast: January 9.

Also Adrian (c.304), a legendary figure who, inspired by the fortitude of Christians under torture at the imperial court of Nicomedia, adopted the faith and joined them in their martyrdom. September 8.

Also a martyr from Batanea who, with his companion Eubulus, died for his faith at Caesarea in 309. March 5.

Also Pope Adrian III, d. 885, who is also venerated as a saint though it is not altogether clear why. He is known, however, to have worked to alleviate the famine in Rome. July 8.

Adrian of May (d. 875) This Hungarian bishop went to Scotland and possibly Ireland as a missionary, retiring to a monastery on the Isle of May in the Firth of Forth where he and his companions were murdered by Danish raiders. Feast: March 4.

Aelred or Ethelred (1110-1067) A preacher and ascetic of great piety and gentleness, he was author of prayers, sermons and *On Spiritual Friendship*. Born in Hexham, England, he became master of the household to King David of Scotland but at 24 became a monk at the Yorkshire Cistercian abbey of Rievaulx, then abbot at Revesby before again returning to Rievaulx as abbot. Feast: February 3.

Agape (d. 304) Burned alive by the Governor of Thessalonika (together with her sisters Chionia and Irene) after being found guilty of possessing Christian texts and refusing to sacrifice to pagan gods. Feast: April 3. *See also* Irene.

Also the name of another martyr who died at either Terni or Antioch and about whom nothing further is known. February 15.

Agatha (date unknown) A Sicilian virgin who early in her life dedicated herself to God and chastity refusing the advances of the consul Quintinian who began to threaten her on account of her Christian faith. She was sent to a brothel, tortured on the rack and had her breasts cut off before being rolled over red hot coals. Her symbols (a pair of pincers and removed breasts presented on a plate) led to the later confusion that they were loaves and was possibly the origin of the blessing of bread on her feast day. Patron of bellfounders, perhaps arising from a similar confusion, and of nurses. She is invoked for protection against fire and future eruptions from Mount Etna. Feast: February 5.

Agatha (d. 1024) The ill-treated spouse of Count Paul of Carinthia, who not only endured his jealousy and ill-treatment but converted him to Christianity and is locally venerated as a model wife. Feast: February 5.

Agnes (d. c.305) She was a young girl of only 13 when she refused marriage, preferring to dedicate herself to Christ. She was martyred, killed by a sword thrust through her throat. One legend says that she was put in a brothel where a man, looking at her naked, was struck blind. Her symbol is a lamb (Latin *agnus*) and the pallia of Catholic archbishops is woven by nuns at a convent of St Agnes from the wool of sheep blessed in Rome. Feast: January 21.

Agnes of Montepulciano (1268-1317) Born in a village near this Tuscan town she was reported to have had visions of Christ, the Virgin and angels and to have effected cures and made prophecies. Entering a convent of the austere Sacchines (Sisters of the Sack – so called on account of their rough habit) at the age of nine and by 15 an abbess by special papal dispensation, she slept on a stone pillow for 15 years, eating only bread and water. She later returned to Montepulciano where a new convent was built for her. After her death from a painful illness her tomb became a place of pilgrimage. Feast: April 20.

Aidan of Lindisfarne (d. 651) First abbot and bishop of Lindisfarne (Holy Island), he brought Christianity to the Northumbria of King Oswald (q.v.). Born in Ireland, he was a monk at Iona before beginning his work at Lindisfarne. Though welcome at the king's table, he embraced poverty, founded churches and used alms to buy slaves their freedom. Feast: August 31.

Alban (c.305) The first British Christian martyr, legend describes him as a Roman soldier born at Verulamium, in Hertfordshire, who, when Christians were being persecuted under Diocletian (or possibly under Septimus Severus c.210, or Decius c.254), sheltered a priest, was converted by him and dressed himself in the priest's clothes to enable him to escape. On arrest, he refused to sacrifice to pagan gods and was sent to be beheaded in the local amphitheatre. The executioner had a miraculous conversion and refused to perform his

duty. The eyes of his replacement, however, are said to have fallen out after he had done the deed. Many cures were reported at Alban's burial place and his shrine attracted many pilgrims, the town of St Albans consequently developing around it. Feast: June 20 (Book of Common Prayer, June 17).

Albert the Great (1206-1280) Doctor of the Church and Bishop of Regensburg, he became a Dominican friar as a teenager, much against the wishes of his family, the counts of Bollstadt on the Danube. Apart from short periods as Prior Provincial of his Order and as bishop (from which he resigned), he studied and taught at Paris, Hildesheim, Regensburg (Ratisbon) and Cologne and wrote widely on science, philosophy and theology, applying Aristotelian methods and adapting the Greek philosopher's works to fit Christian thinking. Feast: November 15.

Alexander (d. 328) A Bishop of Alexandria, he opposed and excommunicated Arius, the propagator of the Arian heresy during his episcopate. Feast: February 26.

Also numerous other saints, including a martyr who died at Alexandria in 250, August 22; one of the martyred Seven Brothers, who shares a feast day with Felicity (q.v.) on July 10; and another martyred at Milan in 397, May 29.

Alexander Nevsky (1220-1263) Prince of Novgorod and defender of Russia against attack by Swedes, Lithuanians, Tartars and Teutonic Knights, he gained his name from his defeat of the Swedes on the banks of the river Neva. Said to have been extremely devout and to have had visions of the martyrs SS Boris and Gleb, he became a monk shortly before his death. Peter the Great made him protector of St Petersburg and he became a symbol of Russian resistance, especially during World War II. Sergei

Eisenstein made a famous film about him, with music by Prokofiev, featuring the Teutons' defeat on frozen Lake Peipus. Feast: November 23.

Alphege (c.953-1012) After a life spent successively as monk, hermit and abbot, he was made bishop of Winchester and was later elevated to the archbishopric of Canterbury. Danish forces captured Canterbury in 1011 and held him for ransom. He refused to pay and forbade others to pay the enormous sum demanded which so annoyed his captors that at Greenwich, after a drunken feast, they beat him very near to death with oxbones, delivering a final blow with an axe. He was buried at St Paul's in London. Feast: April 19.

Ambrose (339-397) Bishop of Milan and one of the four great Doctors of the Church with Augustine, Jerome and Gregory, he was still unbaptized in his mid-thirties when, at the assembly to choose a new bishop, a child's voice was heard to call out 'Ambrose for bishop' and the call was taken up by the crowd. He was an eloquent preacher – said to have been prophesized when he was a baby when a swarm of bees hovered over his mouth – a maker of converts (including Augustine, q.v.), played an important role in Imperial politics and was a major theologian. He composed hymns and encouraged hymn singing, the Ambrosian Rite and Ambrosian Chant being attributed to him, though not necessarily his creation. Feast: December 7 (Book of Common Prayer, April 4).

Anastasia (d. c.304) A Roman matron, she was arrested for helping Christians and put on a slave boat (converting the slaves by her example, for which they were later beheaded) which was guided to land by St Chrysogonus. She was taken to Sirmium on the Danube where she was tied to a St Andrew's cross, had her breasts cut off and was then

beheaded. In the Orthodox Church she is called *Pharmocolytria* because she was believed to make poisons harmless. Feast: December 25 (December 22 in the Eastern Orthodox Church).

Andrew (d. c.60) This simple fisherman was among the first of the apostles of Christ, who promised him that he and his brother Simon Peter would become 'fishers of men'. Traditionally, he is credited with spreading the Gospel in Greece and Scythia and miraculous events are attributed to him such as surviving attacks by wild beasts in the stadium at Thessalonica. At Patras he converted Maximilla, who refused to continue marital relations with her husband, the proconsul, while he remained a pagan. As a result, Andrew was imprisoned, scourged and then crucified by being bound to a cross, on which he took two days to die. In 337, his remains were removed to Byzantium, and, after its conquest by the Crusaders, to Amalfi. In 1461 his head was given to the Pope and was a treasure of the Vatican until returned to the Orthodox Church in Istanbul in 1965. In the 8th century a monk called Regulus had a vision in which he was instructed by an angel to take the relics to Scotland and to build a church at St Andrews. Patron saint of Greece, Russia and Scotland, his cross was originally shown as T-shaped but from the 10th century he is shown with the saltire cross (X) now associated with him. Feast: November 30.

Also numerous other saints, including Andrew of Crete (c.660-740), a monk who became archbishop of Gortyna and a preacher and writer of hymns, whose work still forms part of the Byzantine Liturgy, July 4; Andrew Bobola (1591-1657), a Polish aristocrat who became a Jesuit and was gruesomely killed by Cossacks when he refused to renounce Catholicism. They stripped, scorched and flayed him, cutting off his nose and lips and tearing out his tongue before finally cutting off his head. Feast: May 21.

Andrew Kagwa (d. 1887) Martyr. Feast June 3. *See* Charles Lwanga.

Angelico, Fra (1387-1455) Born Guido di Pietro, at Vicchio, near Florence, he became a friar and produced manuscript illuminations before entering the priesthood. His works include famous murals in the priory of San Marco, Florence, in the Chapel of Nicholas V in the Vatican and in Orvieto cathedral. After Orvieto, he became prior of Fiesole and spent his last years in Rome where he was buried in S. Maria sopra Minerva. A cult soon developed but he was not beatified until 1960. Given further approval in 1982, he was declared the patron saint of artists in 1984. Feast: February 18.

Anne (1st century) She is venerated as the mother of the Blessed Virgin Mary. According to the apocryphal Book of James, her husband Joachim was barred from the temple because he was childless after 20 years of marriage even though the couple still prayed for a child. An angel appeared to them to tell them their prayers had been heard

and when Mary was born she was dedicated to the service of God. Growing devotion to Mary led to an increasing interest in her mother and childless women still pray to her today. Feast: July 25.

Another legend names Mary's parents as Stollanus and Emerentia. Feast: July 26 (July 25 in the East).

Anselm (1033-1109) Was archbishop of Canterbury and a Doctor of the Church, though never formally canonized. Born at Aosta, in Lombardy, he longed to be a monk from boyhood but was prevented by his family. Eventually, he entered the monastery at Bec in Normandy in 1060, soon becoming prior and then abbot. Closely associated with his former teacher Lanfranc, who involved him in the English church, he succeeded him as archbishop of Canterbury thus beginning years of conflict with kings William Rufus and Henry I, though eventually developing close trust with the latter. An important theological writer on such metaphysical subjects as free will and the origin of evil, he was a champion

of the poor and an early opponent of slavery obtaining a resolution, passed at a council in 1107, in which the selling of men as though they were cattle was prohibited. Feast: April 21.

Antony of Egypt (251-356) A hermit, abbot and mystic from Memphis in Upper Egypt, he was still in his teens when, having inherited wealth from his deceased parents, he heard Christ's exhortation to a rich man read in a sermon and followed the call to give everything he had to the poor. In emulation of an old man in the neighbourhood, he assumed the life of a hermit, fasting until sunset and drinking only water. At about 35 years of age he crossed the Nile and lived for nearly 20 years among ruins at the top of a mountain, rarely seeing anyone apart from the man who brought his bread but gaining a great reputation for humility and piety and inspiring others by his example. Round about 305 he abandoned his seclusion to found a monastery at Fayum made up of scattered individual cells where he was followed by others whom he occasionally left his own cell to visit.

He made a trip to Alexandria to encourage those under persecution from Maximinus and made a further visit to preach against the Arians when he is said to have made conversions and worked miracles. In his cell he spent his time in prayer and meditation, wove mats and cultivated a garden but was often visited by temptations which took many forms. His fame spread widely and the Emperor Constantine and his sons wrote beseeching his prayers. He died aged 105 at his cell on Mount Kolzim near the Red Sea after requesting that his burial place should be concealed; but his relics were found in 561 and taken to Alexandria and later elsewhere. Feast: January 17.

Antony of Padua (c.1193-1231) Was a Franciscan preacher and teacher who earned the name 'the hammer of heretics' and to whom numerous miracles were attributed. One of these was said to have occurred when he attempted to preach to the people of Rimini who refused to listen to his sermons. Continuing to preach by the river, the fish leaped out of the water

10

in response to his words and an ass knelt when the Host was raised after a heretic declared he would not believe in the transubstantiation of the Eucharist until his donkey did so. He was adopted as patron saint of Padua, where he died, and intercession is still made to him to find lost possessions. This custom arose because it was said that the thief of a book, either from Antony personally, or from a convent he founded at Brives, was terrified into returning it by an apparition. June 13.

Antony Pechersky (983-1073)
Feast: July 10. *See* Theodosius.

Apollonia (d. c.249) During an anti-Christian riot in Alexandria this elderly deaconess had her teeth broken by her attackers who insisted that she repeated pagan blasphemies or be burned alive. She asked for a moment to consider and then jumped voluntarily into the flames. Artists sometimes depict her as a beautiful young girl having her teeth forcibly extracted and many therefore pray to her for relief from toothache. Feast: February 9. She is sometimes confused with another Apollonia martyred in Rome a century later.

Apphia *See* Philemon.

Athanasius (c.297-373) Bishop of Alexandria, Doctor of the Church, and author of theological works, of which the most important is *Contra Arianos,* an attack on the Arian heresy, he also produced a life of St Antony of Egypt, with whom he was acquainted. Opposition from the Arians (who denied that Christ was consubstantial with God) and others, who from time to time regained Imperial support, exiled him seven times from his diocese - more than a third of his episcopate - years which he spent in Trier, Rome and in the desert. Feast: May 2.

Athanasius the Athonite (c.925-1003) Was abbot of Mount Athos and teacher and author of rules of monastic

life. After teaching in Constantinople he joined a monastery at Kymina in Bithynia, which consisted of monks living in independent cells, but fled to Athos when he suspected that he would be asked to become abbot. Emperor Nicephorus Phocas persuaded him to go to Crete to help organize a successful expedition against the Saracens and was only allowed to return when he agreed to build and head the first organized monastery on Athos where he also constructed the harbour and established a piped water supply. Feast: July 5.

Augustine of Canterbury (d. c.604)

Archbishop and builder of the first cathedral at Canterbury, he was chosen by Gregory the Great to lead a group of missionaries to England where he converted Ethelbert, King of Kent (whose French wife was already Christian), rebuilt an ancient church which became the cathedral and founded the monastery of SS Peter and Paul (later renamed after him). Feast: May 27 (but May 26, the date of his death, in England).

Augustine of Hippo (354-430)

One of the four principle Doctors of the Church, he was author of the *Confessions*, *De Civitate Dei* (The City of God), demonstrating that the Visigoth conquest of Rome was not due to its abandonment of pagan gods, and *De Trinitate*. Born in Numidia (now Algeria) and son of St Monica (q.v.), a Christian, though he was not baptized as a child, he was educated at Carthage and proceeded to Rome and then Milan to teach rhetoric. However his interest in Manichaeism for ten years caused him to renounce Christianity. It was in Milan that the influence of St Ambrose led him towards conversion and, after sending away the woman who had lived with him for many years and borne him a son, he was baptized. Returning to Africa, he spent several years in communal living, teaching, meditating, fasting and praying and, though he had

no previous intention of doing so, was ordained a priest and went to Hippo as assistant to the bishop. There, he established a monastic community and succeeded Valerius as bishop. His controversial teaching on marriage is encapsulated in the preamble to the Anglican Book of Common Prayer and the famous *Te Deum* is said to have been composed by him with St Ambrose. Feast: August 28.

B

Balthasar (1st century)

St Matthew's Gospel tells of wise men, thought to be astrologers from Babylonia or Arabia, who saw a star which heralded Christ's birth and came to pay homage to Him. Traditionally, Balthasar was accompanied by two others, Caspar and Melchior, all referred to either as magi or kings. Feast: July 23.

Barbara (date unknown)

Was said to have been shut in a tower by her father to keep her away from the attentions of suitors. In her father's absence she became a Christian and added a third window, either to her tower or to a bath house, as a symbol of the Trinity thus making it a more suitable place for her to live as a hermit. Her father returned and nearly killed her in his fury, but handed her over to a judge who condemned her to death. As a result, her father was struck by lightning. Another version describes how she was carried by angels from the tower to a secret hideaway. A shepherd who betrayed its location had his flock turned into grasshoppers. After torture and refusal to abjure Christianity, her father beheaded her before being struck by lightning. She has come to be known as patron of those at risk of sudden death by lightning – later by explosive mines and cannon, and of gunsmiths and artillerymen. There is no firm evidence for her existence and she was dropped from the Roman calendar in 1969. Feast day formerly December 4.

LEFT
The Martyrdom of St Bartholomew *by Valentin de Boulogne (1594-1632).*

RIGHT
St Benedict and his Monks Eating in the Refectory *by Il Sodoma (Giovanni Bazzi) (1477-1549), a fresco in the Abbey of Monteoliveto Maggiore, Siena.*

Barnabas (1st century) An early disciple known as an apostle, though not of the twelve. A Jewish Cypriot, he introduced Paul to the Apostles and went with him to Antioch, Cyprus and other places preaching, making converts and sometimes meeting with violence and stoning. The *Acts of the Apostles* mentions him returning to Cyprus and tradition holds that he was stoned to death at Salamis. Feast: June 11.

Bartholomew (1st century)
One of the twelve apostles, his name means 'son of Tolmai' and he and the disciple referred to in St John's Gospel as Nathaniel are thought to be one and the same. Various sources say that he went with Philip to Phrygia or to India where he was flayed and beheaded. The Armenian Church, however, consider him to be their founder because of a belief that he was martyred at the Caspian Sea port of Albanopolis (Derbend). One story says he restored life to the dead son of the Armenian king then drove a devil from him and chained it up. Feast: August 24, celebrated locally at other times.

Basil the Great (c.330-379)
Bishop of Caesarea, Doctor of the Church and Father of the Orthodox Church, he belonged to a family of which grandmother, parents and siblings were all declared saints. He had a brilliant academic career at Caesarea, Constantinople and Athens, developing a student friendship with Gregory of Nazianus and the future emperor Julian the Apostate. He became a monk, however, and was determined to live a life of solitude, settling as a hermit near Caesarea in Asia Minor where he and Gregory frequently preached. He refused Julian's invitations to court and relinquished his hermit life only when called by his bishop to support him against the Arianism of the Emperor Valens, and later became bishop of Caesarea. Famous for his care of the poor he was a champion of the Church's liberties against secular powers but sought control of any abuse within the Church. He set out the rules for monastic life which are still followed in the Eastern Church and were the basis of those devised by St

Benedict (q.v.) in the West. Feast: January 2, January 1 in the East.

Bede, The Venerable (673-735)
A Doctor of the Church, he was first a monk at Jarrow monastery in Northumbria in the north of England, which he entered when he was eight years old. A biblical scholar and historian, his work ranges from lives of the saints to a record of the spread of Christianity in England and a translation of St John's Gospel into the English of his time. He probably never left Northumbria but was respected widely: on his death St Boniface wrote 'the candle of the Church, lit by the Holy Spirit, was extinguished'. The title usually given him of 'venerable' may be derived from a couplet on his shrine: *Haec sunt in fossa/Bedae venerabilis ossa* – 'Here in the grave are the bones of worthy Bede', but his cult as a saint was already established within 50 years of his death. Leo XIII proclaimed him Doctor of the Church in 1899. His feast day was originally May 26 but when this

14

Bénezet (c.1163-1184) A shepherd, originally from Savoy, he was instructed in a vision to bridge the Rhône at Avignon, where he sought support from the bishop, who at first refused to believe him, relenting after Bénezet began work with the help of a few local people. Bénezet died before the bridge was complete and was buried in a chapel built upon it. In 1699, when part of the bridge was washed away, his coffin was rescued and his body was found to be uncorrupted. A folk song has made the bridge at Avignon widely known. Feast: April 14.

Bernadette (1844-1879) Daughter of a poor miller called Soubirous, when she was 14 she had a series of visions at the rock of Massabielle in Lourdes in the foothills of the French Pyrenees, in which a figure describing herself as 'The Immaculate Conception' requested the building of a church and told her to drink from and wash in a spring which gushed from a place below the rock where she was instructed to dig. Bernadette managed to withstand rigorous questioning by both Church and civil authorities but the pressure of attention on this simple peasant so disrupted her life that she decided to become a nun and nursed the wounded of the Franco-Prussian War. Although Lourdes has become a great centre of pilgrimage, claiming many cures, Bernadette herself became very ill and died of tuberculosis when she was only 36. Feast: April 16, but February 18 in France.

Bernard of Clairvaux (1090-1153) A Cistercian abbot and Doctor of the Church, he was born into the Burgundian nobility, and, on account of a dream of a black and white dog (which his mother experienced at his birth) interpreted it to mean that he was destined to become a Benedictine. He duly joined the Order at Cîteux once his studies in Paris were over. The strict interpretation of its Benedictine rule eventually earned the

became the feast of Thomas Becket (q.v.) it was changed to May 27 (in the Roman Church since 1969, May 25).

Benedict (c.480-c.550) Author of the Rule of the Benedictine Order and patriarch of Western monasticism, he was born of a noble family of Nursia and sent to Rome to be educated. But he soon rejected the worldliness of life and strongly felt the call to be a hermit. In the wild and rocky countryside in what is now Subiaco he isolated

himself in a mountain cave to which he hauled up food each day provided by the monk Romanus. Here, his asceticism and tales of his being a miracle worker attracted disciples and he set up a series of twelve monasteries around the place. Then he suddenly abomdoned the area – there are stories of jealousies and an attempt on his life – and on the site of an ancient hill-top temple near Naples built chapels and established the famous abbey of Monte Cassino, the monks all being gathered in one

establishment. Here, influenced by St Basil and other monastic leaders, he completed the final version of his Rule which required prayer, sacred reading, manual labour and obedience. It was further developed and the Order later offered its hospitality, as well as medical, educational and agricultural skills to the world. Despite all this, Benedict was never himself a priest. Formerly March 21, his feast day was transferred by the Roman Church to July 11, in 1969, to ensure it falls outside Lent.

order the appellation Cistercian. In 1115 he moved with a group of monks to Clairvaux where he established a new Cistercian monastery and continued to maintain this strict rule. The reputation of Clairvaux and its abbot attracted many who wished to be monks and led to the foundation of other Cistercian houses in France, Britain and Ireland. Although it was a secluded Order, Bernard's advice and support were sought in wider Church affairs including the cause of Innocent II, the recognition of the Knights Templar, the suppression of the Albigensian heresy and the preaching,of the disastrous Second Crusade. He intervened in the appointment of bishops and opposed the opinions of scholars such as Peter Abelard. His influence was enormous and he was treated as a saint in his own lifetime being actually canonized less than 20 years after his death.
Feast: August 20.

Bernardino of Siena (1380-1444)
Son of the governor of Masadi Carrera but orphaned and reared by aunts, he was sent to Siena for his education and there joined a group nursing victims of the plague. A vision instructed him to care for souls as well as bodies and he gave away his possessions and became a Franciscan in 1402 and one of the Osservanti, a particularly strict branch of the Order, in the following year. After living and studying in retirement and preaching only occasionally, in 1417 in Milan, he began a life of preaching. He developed his voice to address huge crowds for three or four hours at a time and travelled on foot to preach in all the states of Italy, except Naples, becoming vicar-general of the Osservanti in 1437. He established schools of theology for the Observants, who had previously ignored scholarship, and probably wrote a set of statutes for the Order before resigning and returning to preaching in 1443. His poor health now made it necessary to travel by donkey and he died the

following year on his way to preach in Naples. His sermons were enlivened with humour and mimicry and he would hold up for veneration a plaque bearing the letters *IHS* surrounded by rays with a Latin quotation of John 17: 6 – 'I have manifested thy name unto the people'. This brought accusations that he was encouraging

idolatry and trial by the Inquisition. His acquittal encouraged the wider use of this symbol of the Holy Name of Jesus. Feast: May 20.

Blaise (d. c.316) In later life he was a bishop of Sebastea in Armenia and unsubstantiated 8th-century accounts say that he was a martyr of the

persecution of Licinius. During the earlier persecution under Diocletian he hid in a cave in a forest where wild animals brought him food and he blessed any that were sick or wounded. Hunters seeing this, and thinking he was a magician, threw him in prison, where he saved the life of a boy choking on a fish bone. The boy's

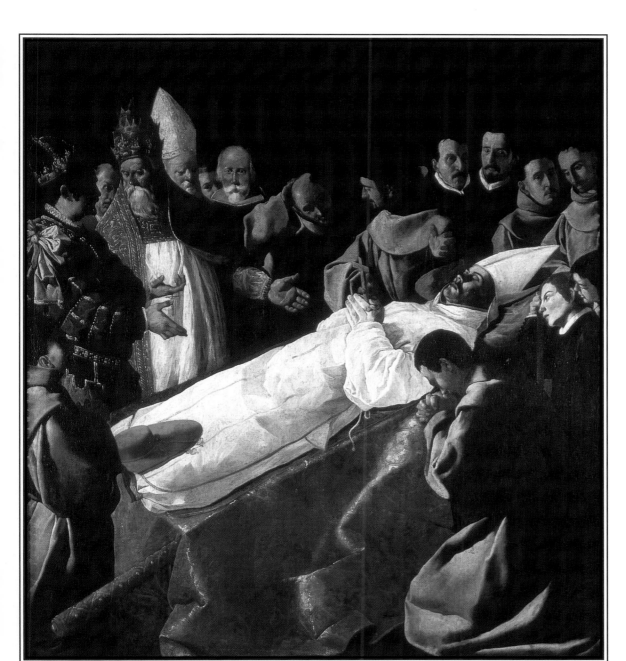

the Poverty of Christ. Made Minister-General of the Order in 1257, his diplomacy helped create a temporary reunion of the Roman and Orthodox Churches at the Council of Lyons in 1274, the year after he became cardinal-archbishop of Albano. He wrote a life of St Francis which was declared official, all others being destroyed. He promoted study and teaching as important roles for friars, thereby requiring libraries and buildings, which conflicted with St Francis's views on possessions. Feast: July 15 (formerly July 14).

Boniface (680-754) Archbishop and martyr, this Benedictine monk from Devon who became a missionary in Germany was later made archbishop of Mainz. At Geismar he cut down an oak sacred to pagan gods and their failure to wreak revenge or to protect their followers helped boost Christian conversions. He founded schools and monasteries and carried out reforms concerning the discipline of clergy in both France and Germany. He was murdered by pagans while preparing for a confirmation service on the banks of the Borne near Dokkum. Feast: June 5.

Brendan (c.486-c.575) This Irish abbot founded monasteries at Clonfert

mother brought candles in thanks (thus forever linking the event to the practice of applying candles to sore throats) and asked his blessing. His flesh was torn with metal combs before he was beheaded, hence his patronage of wool-combers. Feast: February 3.

Bonaventure (c.1218-1274) In later life a cardinal and Doctor of the Church and known as the 'Seraphic Doctor', he became a Franciscan in his early twenties and was sent to Paris to study, becoming a teacher there himself and Master of the Franciscan school. His reply to secular attempts to have the friars excluded from the Paris schools was encapsulated in Concerning

in western Ireland and elsewhere, travelling through Wales, Scotland and perhaps Brittany as a missionary. His travels which earned him the title 'The Navigator' occasioned a 9th-century romance in which he sails west from Kerry for seven years to discover the 'Isles of the Blessed'. Feast: May 16.

Bridget or Birgitta (1303–1373)

Married at 14 and mother of eight (one being St Catherine of Sweden), on widowhood she adopted the life of a penitent. She had, however, as a lady-in-waiting to the Swedish queen, already had many of the dreams and visions which she was later to record in her *Revelations*. She made pilgrimages to Rome, Assisi and other Italian shrines and to the Holy Land and founded the Brigettine order. Patron of Sweden. Feast: July 23 (Formerly October 8).

Brigid or Bride (d. c.525)

Said to have been baptized as a young peasant girl by St Patrick himself, she later became a nun and founded a monastery at Kildare, Ireland, where she became abbess and helped spread the Faith. Legends which sprang up about her echo Irish pagan lore and biblical incidents and she is credited with such feats as turning water into beer, encouraging cows to provide miraculous quantities of milk and multiplying supplies of food to feed the poor. Patron of poets, blacksmiths and healers. Feast: February 1.

Brigid or Britt (5th century)

Scottish princess who, with her sister Maura, was murdered in Picardy while on a pilgrimage to Rome. Feast: November 2.

Bruno (c.1032–1101)

Founder of the Carthusian Order, he was the son of a noble family of Cologne and was educated in Rheims where he also taught for many years and was instrumental in bringing charges against its scandalous archbishop. By then, he had decided to become a monk and, after a period as a hermit near Moslesme, moved to La Grande Chartreuse in the mountains near Grenoble where bishop St Hugh made land available to him for a new foundation. Here, he and six of his companions built an oratory and individual cells, the first of the Carthusian monasteries (or Charterhouses as they came to be known in English). The monks lived an austere life of prayer, study and manual work. The physical tasks were later assumed by lay brothers freeing the

monks for their main occupation of copying manuscripts. After six years, Pope Urban (who had been Bruno's student in Rheims) summoned him to Rome as his adviser and he made himself a hermit's cell in the ruins of the baths of Diocletian. Bruno refused an archbishopric but was not, however, allowed to return to Chartreuse. Instead, he founded another monastery at La Torre in Calabria within easier reach of Rome. He was never formally canonized, Carthusians shunning such publicity, but the Order was given leave to keep his feast day which was later extended to the whole Church. Feast: October 6.

C

Cadfan (5th century) A Breton-born abbot who founded a monastery on Bardsey Island and a church at Towyn in Wales where there was a holy well said to cure rheumatism and skin conditions. Feast: November 1.

Caedmon (d. 680) As an illiterate herdsman, he was commanded in a dream to 'sing of the beginning of created things'. He awoke to find that he had received the gift of poetry and song thus becoming one of the earliest English poets. He transformed bible stories into brilliant vernacular verse of which only nine lines survive in Bede's *Ecclesiastical History*. He became a monk at the local Whitby Abbey, leading a saintly life of piety and holiness. Feast: February 11.

Cajetan (1480-1547) Italian founder of the Theatine Order, he was born in Vicenza and educated at Padua in theology and law where he decided to become a priest. He was later responsible for setting up fraternities devoted to workers and the service of the sick and poor. In 1523, with the future Pope Paul IV (then bishop of Theate), he founded a new order of clergy who sought to model their lives on those of the Apostles. In Naples he set up the *montes pietatis*, pawn shops designed to help the poor rather than

exploit them. Miracles were claimed by those seeking his intercession. Feast: August 7.

Callixtus (d. 222) A slave in early life who, having mismanaged a bank for his Christian master, was sentenced to work on a treadmill. Released, he was involved in a brawl in a synagogue, possibly attempting to reclaim debts for the bank's investors, and was sent to work in Sardinian mines. Eventually, and by now a freeman, he was put in charge of a Christian burial ground where the early popes were interred. In 217 he was elected pope. His policies, which included allowing repentant murderers and adulterers to take communion and permitting marriages between slaves and free men and women, which were against Roman law, led to a split in the church. Even though he died in a riot, he is considered by many to have died a martyr. Feast: October 14.

Canute (d. 1086) The bastard great-nephew of King Canute, who was also king of England, he gained the Danish throne in 1081 and made unsuccessful attempts to invade England and claim its crown. He was killed by rebels, led by his brother Olaf, while kneeling before the altar in St Alban's church, Odensee, having just received the Sacrament. Patron of Denmark. Feast: January 19.

Casimir (1458-1484) A Polish prince, the devout youth, when aged 13, was given to the penitential wearing of a hair shirt. He was chosen by alienated Hungarian nobles to replace their monarch. He reluctantly accepted and led an army against the ruling king, his father. The size of the opposing force and desertions from their own ranks caused his soldiers to advise him against this course of action and he was confined on his return to the castle of Dobzki. He adopted a life of celibacy and austerity and refused to take part in war with any Christian kingdom when all were in danger from the Turks. Feast: March 4.

Caspar *See* Balthasar.

Castalus *See* Sebastian.

Catherine of Alexandria (4th century) Possibly mythical, she was said to have been a Christian Egyptian princess who the Virgin Mary, in a vision to a hermit, described as a mystic 'bride of Christ'. She took up the cause of Christians persecuted by the Emperor Maxentius, disputing with 50 philosophers called in to shake her faith whom she converted, along with the Empress and her servants. All were executed, except Catherine, after whom Maxentius lusted and wished to marry. She refused, declaring that she was already betrothed to Christ, and was condemned to death on a spiked wheel (the origin of the Catherine Wheel). This was shattered by angels or lightning from heaven and she was beheaded, milk instead of blood

flowing from her veins. Her body is said to have been carried by angels to Mount Sinai where it was discovered late in the 8th century. She is patron of students, philosophers, children's nurses, wheelwrights, spinners and millers. Feast: November 25 until 1969 when, despite being known as one of the Fourteen Holy Helpers, veneration to her as a saint was suppressed.

Catherine of Bologna (1413-1463) Author of a book of prophesies, she had a vision one Christmas of the Virgin Mary who placed the Christ child in her arms. A member of the order of Poor Clares, she was buried in her own convent. Patron of Bologna. Feast: March 9.

Catherine of Genoa (1447-1510) A visionary and mystic, she was 16 when her family arranged her marriage to an unfaithful and profligate husband

who cared nothing for her, was never at home and made her life wretched; her loneliness, however, increased her religious fervour. The loss of his fortune and her constant prayers later led to her husband's reformation and thereafter the couple lived humble and celibate lives caring for the sick, including the victims of Genoa's plague in 1493. Catherine died with fortitude after suffering an agonizing illness. Patron of Genoa. Feast: September 13.

Catherine of Siena (c.1347-1380)

The devout daughter of a dyer and a future Doctor of the Church, she became, at the age of 14, a member of the Dominican Third Order, living in seclusion at home and leaving it only to tend the sick. In 1366, she had a vision in which the Virgin Mary took her hand and Christ placed a ring upon her finger. Thereafter, she ventured out into the world, attracting disciples and the attention of those seeking her advice and later intervening in Church affairs. She is renowned for her letters and other spiritual texts even though she could not write herself and would have needed to dictate them. In 1375, while meditating on the Crucifixion, she received the stigmata on her hands and feet. Patron of Siena. Feast: April 30, April 29 since 1969.

Cecilia (2nd or 3rd century)

This Roman girl agreed to marry on her father's orders but insisted that her husband Valerian respect her vow of perpetual virginity on pain of punishment by her guardian angel. He agreed, provided he could see the angel, who appeared to them on his baptism, presenting crowns of roses and lilies. Valerian's brother, Tiburtius, was also converted and later imprisoned for preaching Christianity. But they converted their jailor and all three were beheaded. After their burial, Cecilia was prevailed upon to sacrifice to pagan gods and when she refused was sentenced to be executed in her steam bath, the furnace of which was stoked

20

up to an abnormal degree. When this failed, they tried to behead her and failed three times sujecting her to a lingering death. There is no historic evidence for Cecilia's existence and her story first appeared towards the end of the 5th century; but in 817, Pope Paschal I had a vision which guided him to her supposed sarcophagus. When it was opened in 1599, the still uncorrupted body of a beautiful woman was found. The Academy of Music in Rome chose her as their patron when it was founded in 1584 and she is now revered as the patron saint of music. Feast: November 22.

Chad (d. 672) A Northumberland-born disciple of Aidan, he was made abbot of Lastingham and subsequently bishop of York on the instructions of King Oswin when another candidate should have been more properly appointed. A new Archbishop of Canterbury removed him from the post but was so impressed by his humility and sanctity that he arranged for him to become bishop of Lichfield, ordering that the aged Chad should henceforth travel on horseback. Feast: March 2.

Charity *See* Sophia.

Charles Borromeo (1538–1584) A cardinal priest of the Church and important figure of the counter-Reformation, he was born of an aristocratic family and was a nephew of the Medici Pope Pius IV. He became a monk at the age of 12 and received the income from the family abbey at Arona. As a student at Milan and Pavia he was hampered by a speech impediment but after his uncle became pope he was given a succession of important posts and played a major role in organizing the Council of Trent and promulgating subsequent reforms. He became head of the family at 23 when his brother died and many expected him to resume secular life and marry; but instead, he resigned his family

position, became a priest and was made bishop of Milan. It was not, however, until after Pius' death that he was allowed to reside in his diocese. He endeavoured to live a simple life, giving much of his wealth to the poor and the English College at Douai. He personally helped feed the hungry and tend the sick of Milan during outbreaks of famine and plague, giving last rites to the dying. Patron of Bologna. Feast: November 4.

Charles Garnier (1605–1649) Jesuit martyr. Feast: October 19. *See* Isaac Jogues.

Charles Lwanga (d. 1887) Charles and his companions are together known as the martyrs of Uganda. He was the eldest of a group of 20 young men and boys – the youngest being 13-year-old Kizito

and none older than 25 – who were all canonized in 1964. They were rolled in reed mats and burned alive by a fanatically anti-Christian ruler called Mwanga. The wave of persecution which had already killed Joseph Mkasa and Denis Seebuggwawo (q.v.) spread to include Chief Andrew Kagwa, chief of the Kigowa, and Matthias Murumba. Feast: June 3 for all these martyrs.

Christina (4th century) Virgin martyr. Probably from Bolsena, in Tuscany, she was martyred with arrows like St Sebastian after tortures involving millstones, a wheel and pincers. The shrine and catacomb associated with her survive even though Christina may not have been her actual name. Feast: July 24.

An identical story which combines elements of the stories of SS Barbara, Catherine and Ursula, is also attributed to Christine of Tyre in Phoenicia who probably never existed. Later historical Christinas include a Saxon girl who managed to maintain her virginity, despite a marriage which was eventually annulled, and who lived as a hermit, and the 13th-century Christina the Astonishing who, thought to be dead after suffering a fit, sat up at her funeral and rose to the beams of the church, later claiming to have been to hell, purgatory and heaven before coming back to life. She appeared to be impervious to fire and cold and went to great lengths to avoid the smell of people ending her life in a convent. All their feast days are on July 24.

Christopher (3rd century?) He was supposedly a Canaanite giant who, having been baptized, was instructed to serve travellers by carrying them across a river. Once, carrying a child, he found the weight unaccountably heavy. The child explained that he was Christ and that Christopher (Christ-bearer) had been carrying the weight of the world and its Maker. As proof of this he was told to plant his staff in the ground where it burst into blossom the next day. Christopher went on to preach in Lycia but was imprisoned when he refused to make pagan sacrtifices. Prostitutes sent to his prison to corrupt him were instead converted by him. He was beaten with iron rods, shot at with arrows which missed (though one struck the king's eye – later healed by Christopher's blood), and was eventually beheaded. Patron of travellers, he is also invoked for protection against flood, tempest and plague. His popularity among modern motorists and travellers did not prevent the Vatican, however, from reducing his festival to local cult status in 1969.
Feast: July 25.

Chrysostom (*see* John Chrysostom)

Clare (1194-1253) Founder of the Poor Clares, she was born in Assisi in 1211 where she responded to the preaching of St Francis by sacrificing all her possessions to become a nun. She founded a community of women next to the Church of San Damiano living according to the Franciscan Rule. Though her nuns founded convents in other countries, she never left the walls of San Damiano. Patron of television. Feast: August 11.

Clement (d. c.100) Author of an epistle to the Corinthians and others he is said to have been exiled from Rome to work in the mines of the Crimea where he miraculously caused a spring to flow. He was martyred by drowning, an anchor being tied around his neck. His remains, complete with anchor were supposedly found by SS Cyril and Methodius (q.v.). Patron of Trinity House, the British lighthouse authority. Feast: November 23 (November 24 in East).

Columba or Columcille (c.521-597) An Irish monk, born into the royal O'Neill clan, he founded

St Clement Striking the Rock Below the Holy Lamb *by Bernardino Fungai (1460-1516).*

RIGHT

St Basil (right) with SS Gregory Nazianus (left) and John Chrysostom (centre), the evangelists of Cappadocia, a Byzantine icon of the 17th century.

monasteries at Derry, Durrow and probably Kells before going with a group of twelve others to create a monastery on the small Scottish island of Iona in the Inner Hebrides. From here he carried out missionary work in Scotland and northern England and founded churches in Inverness. Three surviving Latin poems may be part of his literary output and a psalter known as the *Cathach of Columba* is an example of his skill as a scribe. Iona became a leading centre of Celtic Christianity and a burial place for Scottish, Irish and Scandinavian kings. Feast: June 9.

Constantine (d. c.576) Traditionally a king who became a monk and the first Scottish martyr at Kintyre, the same name and story are also placed in Ireland and in Cornwall describing him as a local chief turned monk and founder of churches. Feast in Scotland, March 11; in Cornwall and Wales, March 9.

Constantine the Great (d. 337) The son of St Helena, he was first acclaimed joint Roman Emperor in York, England following his father's death, and was confirmed after defeating his rival in battle in 312. This followed a vision in which he saw a cross in the sky superimposed

LEFT

SS Cosmas and Damian *by Fernando del Rincon (late 15th century). The doctor saints in a piece of miraculous surgery replace a wounded man's leg with that of a dead black man whose body with the exchanged white leg attached is in the foreground.*

upon the sun and heard a voice say 'in this sign conquer'. He formally recognized Christianity as a religion within the Empire and sought to use it in the service of the state. His intervention at the Council of Nicea ensured the defeat of the Arian heresy and he made Sunday a public holiday to facilitate worship. With his mother he built and endowed many churches, though he was not himself baptized until shortly before his death. He caused Byzantium to be rebuilt and made it his capital as Constantinople in 330. Feast: May 21 (In the East only).

Cosmas and Damian (date unknown)
Legend describes them as twin Arabs from Cilicia in Asia Minor, skilled surgeons who gave their services free of charge. It is said that they were raised as Christians at Cyrrhusa in about 287 during the Diocletian persecution. Refusing to sacrifice to pagan gods, they were thrown into the sea, rescued by angels, burned without coming to harm, stoned (the stones returning to strike their persecutors), and finally beheaded. Patrons of medical doctors. Feast: September 26 (formerly 27); in the East, July 1 or November 1.

Crispin and Crispianus (d. c.290) According to French tradition they were Romans sent to spread the Gospel to Gaul. They are said to have preferred to work as shoemakers rather than rely on charity. Alternatively, they are said to have made shoes free of charge, angels bringing them fresh leather every night. Possibly martyred at Soissons, where their cult developed in the 6th century, they were beheaded after surviving stabbing with awls and thrown into the river weighted with millstones. Another version of their story describes them escaping to England and working as cobblers at Faversham near Canterbury. Patrons of shoemakers and leatherworkers. Feast: October 25.

Cunegud (c.978-1033)
Wife of the Holy Roman Emperor Henry II she became a Benedictine nun on his death, devoting herself to prayer, study and the care of the sick. Feast: March 3.

Cuthbert (c.634-687) A Saxon from Northumberland, he had a vision of angels carrying a soul to heaven the night St Aidan died at nearby Bamborough. Later, he became a monk at Melrose Abbey where he was elected prior and was engaged in missionary work before becoming prior

at Lindisfarne. While there, he lived for a time as a hermit on an adjacent island (St Cuthbert's Isle) and on resigning his office transferred to a more remote hermitage on Inner Farne. Pressed to accept a bishopric, he eventually agreed to Durham but arranged an exchange so that he could became bishop of Lindisfarne. He was said to possess healing gifts in life and the same miraculous powere are also attributed to his shrine.
Feast: March 20.

Cyprian and Justina (c.300)

Cyprian was a magistrate of Antioch and Justina the Christian with whom he fell in love. Legend says he sold his soul to the devil for help in seducing her but was saved when she converted him instead. Another version describes him as a necromancer employed by a man in love with Justina who came to desire her himself. After surviving immersion in a pot of boiling pitch the couple were sent to Nicomedia and were beheaded there. Feast: September 25, suppressed in 1969.

Cyricus and Julitta or Cyr and Giulietta (d. c.300)

This three-year-old and his mother fled from Iconium to Tarsus to escape persecution but were recognized. The mother was about to be beheaded (or sawn in two in another version) when her son ran forward shouting that he was a Christian, too. Both were said to have been killed at the same moment (some versions say after a series of tortures which caused the perpetrators to suffer as much as their victims) and fountains sprang from their blood. Feast: June 16; June 15 in the East.

Cyril of Alexandria (c.376-444)

A bishop and Doctor of the Church, this Alexandrian theologian led the case for the doctrine of the Trinity against Nestorius, Archbishop of Constantinople, and his supporters (who believed that there were two parts, God and Man being united in Christ by only a moral union), and established the Virgin Mary as

28

Theotokos (Mother of God) as a tenet of orthodoxy. Feast: June 27 (formerly February 9 or January 28). In the East, June 9.

Cyril of Jerusalem (c.315-386)

Archbishop, Doctor of the Church and author of a series of discourses on the catechism, he was for many years exiled from his Jerusalem episcopacy for opposition to the Arian bishop Acacius who challenged him both on procedural and doctrinal points and accused him of selling Church property. This he did, however, to help the poor during a famine, for which there was good precedent. At the second ecumenical Council of Constantinople in 381 he supported the revised Nicene Creed.
Feast: March 18.

Cyril (c.826-869) and Methodius (c.815-885)

Known as the 'Apostles of the Slavs', they were two brothers from Thessalonica. Cyril, who was baptized Constantine and adopted Cyril only on becoming a monk shortly before his death, became librarian at Santa Sophia. Methodius, after a short period as governor of a Slav colony, became a monk. In 863 they were sent out, with assistants, as missionaries to Moravia. As well as converting and preaching, they produced a script in which Slavonic could be written – the Glagolitic alphabet – from which the Cyrillic characters of Russian were later derived. They met with fierce opposition from German missionaries who particularly objected to their using a vernacular liturgy and the German bishop refused to ordain priests from among their converts. Called to Rome, they took with them the relics of St Clement, discovered by Cyril in the Crimea, where Cyril later became a monk and died. Methodius became archbishop of Sirmium and, after being coerced into giving up the vernacular liturgy, archbishop of Moravia. They are joint patrons of Europe.
Feast: February 14 (formerly March 9 or July 7); in the East, May 11.

D

Damian *See* Cosmas.

Daniel (409-493)

A monk from the age of 12, he was greatly impressed, on a visit to Antioch, by Simon Stylites. Refusing the post of abbot at his own monastery, he returned to Antioch and climbed up to receive instruction from Simon, planning to go to Palestine but prevented from doing so by becoming a hermit near Constantinople. Communicating through only a small window he remained there for nine years but, after the death of Simon Stylites, set himself up on a pillar overlooking the Bosphorous. This was so exposed that he nearly froze to death and the Emperor replaced it with a pair of pillars which supported a balustraded perch which afforded some shelter. Here he prayed, preached, gave advice

and healed the sick for 33 years. When he died his hair was 4 cubits long, a cubit being the distance from the elbow to the tip of the middle finger; his beard measured 3 cubits. Feast: December 11.

David or Dewi (6th century)

Primate of Wales and one of the Seven Champions, he was first mentioned administering the Mass in an 8th-century Irish text. But of his earlier life, apart from a document written in an attempt to establish Wales as outside the jurisdiction of Canterbury, there are no reliable sources. He is said to have been the son of King Sant of southern Wales and a monk who founded several monasteries where strict asceticism was practised and only water drunk. The most famous was at Menevia or Mynyw on the Dyfed (Pembrokeshire) coast, now known as St David's. He is also said to have founded the monastery at

Glastonbury. One of the privations he practised was immersion in cold water. Feast: March 1.

Denis (d. c.250) Bishop of Paris and its patron saint, he was Italian-born but sent as a missionary to Gaul, making many converts around Paris where he was arrested, together with his deacon St Eleutherius and his priest St Rusticus. All three were beheaded and thrown into the Seine. But the bodies were recovered and a chapel built over their tomb which became the abbey of Saint-Denis. He was also known as Dionysius and later confused with an earlier martyr of the same name who was the first bishop of Athens and who was baptized by St Paul. Feast: October 9.

Denis Seebuggwawo (d. 1887) Martyr. Feast: June 3. *See* Charles Lwanga.

Didymus (d. c.304) *See* Theodora.

Dominic (1170-1221) Founder of the Black Friars, this Spanish priest and prior, although not actively involved in the persecution of the Albigensians of southern France, organized a group of women and preachers to teach and try to reconcile these heretics to the Roman Church, thus laying the foundations of his Order. By accepting poverty and a rule based on the teaching of St Augustine, he abandoned manual labour concentrating instead on scholarship, teaching and preaching. The Order later provided missionaries to Asia and America. Dominic travelled widely, was a fine administrator and provided theological advice to the Inquisition. While St Francis promoted the faith by emphasis on the love of God, Dominic used rational argument:

their joint efforts were symbolized when they met and exchanged the Kiss of Peace. Feast: August 8 (formerly August 6).

Dorothy (d. c.313) Legend tells how, when she was being led to execution as a martyr, a young lawyer called Theophilus mockingly asked her to send him some of the fruits of the Garden of Paradise. As she knelt and prayed before her death, an angel appeared with three apples and three roses. These were sent to Theophilus who himself became a Christian and was later martyred. Feast: formerly February 6.

Dunstan (909-988) A Benedictine monk from early manhood and for a time a hermit at Glastonbury, he spent time at the royal court before King Edmund made him abbot there. He rebuilt the monastery and made Glastonbury an important seat of learning. After Edmund's murder he became adviser to King Edred who left part of his treasure at Glastonbury. An advocate of moral reform in both Church and State, his criticism of the next teenage king's behaviour – leaving his coronation banquet for an assignation with a woman and her daughter – led to his disgrace and exile. But he was recalled by the next king, Edgar, who created him, in succession, bishop of Worcester and of London and Archbishop of Canterbury. His exile provided him with experience of the continental Church which influenced his monastic and church reforms and he contributed to the formulation of Edgar's laws. A metalworker and illuminator of some skill, he also played the harp and composed hymns.

Patron of jewellers, goldsmiths, blacksmiths, locksmiths and armourers. Feast: May 19.

Dympna (7th century?) The daughter of a widowed British or Irish chief, she was forced to flee his incestuous attentions. At Gheel, near Antwerp, she, together with her confessor St Gerebernus and two companions, built an oratory and lived as hermits. Her father, however, managed to trace them and when she refused to return with him cut off her head, his men killing the others. After the bodies were discovered in the 13th century, many cures of epilepsy and madness were reported. Gheel has since become a pioneering centre for

the treatment of the mentally ill. Patron of the insane. Feast: May 15.

E

Edmund (841–870) At the age of 14 he was elected king of the East Angles, and then of Suffolk in 856. He ruled well but in about 869 faced invasion by Danes who, having taken York, conquered their way into Norfolk where Edmund fought them and was captured. It was demanded that he gave up his faith and become a vassal king; but he refused to do either and was executed in their traditional way by being tied to a tree and scourged, then shot by arrows before being beheaded, or spreadeagled. First buried where he

died at Hoxne, his body was taken to Bedricsworth early in the 10th century, which became known as Bury St Edmund's (meaning St Edmund's Borough, though it had also become his burial place). Feast: November 20.

Edmund Campion (1540–1581) An eloquent and popular Oxford academic, he gained the patronage of Elizabeth I and was ordained in the Church of England even though he was somewhat ambivalent towards Protestantism. He avoided the necessity of taking up a firm position by going to Dublin where he helped found its university. But, in 1571, he made his way to the English College, re-entering the Roman Church and becoming a

Jesuit two years later. As a Jesuit priest he was sent back to England disguised as a jewel merchant and travelled the country secretly, succouring Catholic prisoners, preaching to recusants and printing treatises. He was arrested preaching at a house in Wantage in Berkshire, taken to the Tower of London and tortured before being tried on a charge of plotting and inciting rebellion. He claimed to be still a loyal subject of the Queen but was hung, drawn and quartered at Tyburn. Feast: October 25.

Edward the Confessor (1003–1066) Sent to Normandy to escape the Danish occupation of the throne in 1013, he became king of England in 1042.

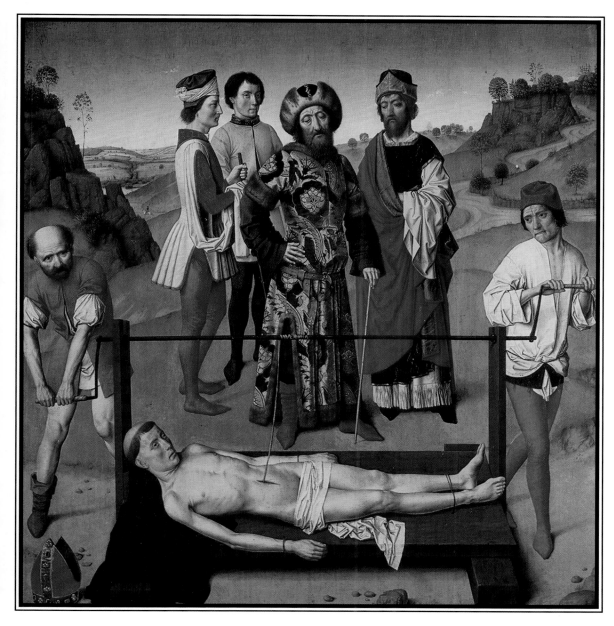

Variously described as a weak or a good king, he maintained peace in the kingdom, despite contention between Saxon and Norman factions, and, after naming the Saxon Harold as his successor, turned much of his attention to religion and the building of St Peter's Abbey at Westminster. During his life he had a reputation for holiness, was said to have seen visions, to have cured scrofula by touch and was thought not to have consummated marriage with his queen. He was too ill to attend the consecration of Westminster Abbey but was buried there. The title Confessor was given by Pope Alexander III in 1161 in token of Edward's saintly life when he was canonized. Feast: originally January 5, but replaced by October 13, the date of his translation.

Edward the Martyr (c.963-979)
Chosen king of England in 975 with the support of St Dunstan, though his stepmother wished her own son to succeed, he was murdered when hunting three years later. His sainthood is based on miraculous cures associated with his remains, first buried at Wareham and then translated to a nunnery at Shaftesbury.
Feast: March 18.

Egbert (d. 729) A Northumbrian monk of particular holiness and erudition, he began his religious life at Lindisfarne and thence went to Ireland where he vowed to remain in voluntary exile for life if he recovered from the plague. A vision directed him to Iona where, from 716, he succeeded in persuading the monastery to adopt the Roman liturgy and fix the date of Easter according to that rather than Celtic rites. Feast: April 24.

Eleutherius (d. 532)
Was made bishop of Tournai, his native city, in 486, and many pagans and heretics were converted by his preaching. A young girl fell in love with him and fell ill and passed into a coma when he would have nothing to do with her. Eleutherius told her father that he would restore her to health on condition that he became a Christian. However, the father refused to keep his promise and Eleutherius brought plague to the land which resulted in the father repenting and believing.
Feast: February 20.

Eligius or Eloi (c.590-c.660)
This Limousin goldsmith was called to Paris to make a throne for Clotaire I. He managed to make two from the metal allotted, earning the friendship of the king and more commissions, eventually becoming master of the Paris mint. His wealth and influence enabled him to ransom slaves, build churches and monasteries and support the poor. A counsellor and diplomat at the court of Clotaire's son, Dagobert I, he was later ordained becoming bishop of Noyon and Tournai in 641 where he concentrated his ministry in the surrounding locality as well as in Flanders. Patron of goldsmiths, blacksmiths and farriers.
Feast: December 1.

Elizabeth (1st century) Mother of John the Baptist, kinswoman of the Virgin Mary and wife of Zacharius, she was visited by the Archangel Gabriel who announced that she would bear a child despite her advanced years. She is said to have escaped the Massacre of the Innocents by fleeing with her child into the desert where a rock opened up to hide them until the danger was over. Feast: November 5.

Elizabeth of Hungary (1207-1231) The daughter of Andrew II of Hungary and happily married to Louis IV, Landgrave of Thuringia, she was a benefactor of orphans, hospitals and the poor and was devastated when Louis died of plague while on a Crusade to the Holy Land. Driven from court by her brother-in-law and refusing to remarry she joined the Franciscan Third Order. Devoid of ostentation and with a confessor who had been a former inquisitor of heretics who slapped and beat her, she cared for the sick and the poor, spinning thread, catching fish for them and even cleaning their houses. The rigours of such a life caused her early death at only 24. Feast: originally November 19, now 17.

Elizabeth Seton (1774-1821) Founder of the American Sisters of Charity, the first Catholic religious society in the United States, she was originally an Episcopalian engaged in social work, helping to found the Society for the Relief of Poor Widows with Small Children in 1794. She was on a visit to Italy, where they had gone because of her husband's health, when he died leaving her with five children. On returning to America she converted to Catholicism and was encouraged to start a school in Baltimore (the first of many) and establish a small religious community. This was approved by the archbishop of Baltimore as the American Sisters of Charity, and she took vows and became its superior the following year. Since then it has grown into a large and influential Order. Elizabeth was the first native-born American citizen to be canonized. Feast: January 4.

Elmo or Erasmus (d. c.300) This future bishop and martyr was a Syrian who, fleeing the persecution of Diocletian, was fed by a raven on Mount Lebanon. The Archangel Michael commanded him to spread the Gospel in Italy where he became bishop of Formiae and was subsequently martyred. Other versions of the story say that he was captured on the mountain, beaten, rolled in pitch and set on fire. Surviving, he was twice released from prison by angelic intervention and taken to Formiae. Because he preached in a thunderstorm, fearless of the lightning around him, his name was linked to the electrical discharge sometimes seen around the rigging of boats after storms and thereafter called St Elmo's Fire and his angelic journey across the Mediterranean forms yet another link with sailors and the sea. The maritime connection may explain his emblem of a windlass but it could also refer to the manner of his martyrdom for it is said that one was used to remove the entrails from his body. Patron of sailors, protector from seasickness and bowel disorders. Feast: June 2.

Ermenburga (d. c.700) This Kentish princess was founder and abbess of a foundation at Minster on the isle of Thanet, on land given as blood-payment by King Egbert for the murder by one of his counsellors of her brothers Ethelred and Ethelbricht, who themselves were celebrated locally as martyrs at Ramsey and Canterbury during the Middle Ages. Feast day formerly celebrated on February 13. *See also* Mildred.

Eugenia (d. c.257) According to legend she was the daughter of a Roman governor of Egypt who ran away from home disguised as a man, was baptized, and joined a monastery of which she became abbess. Her secret was discovered when a woman she cured and whose advances she rejected accused her of adultery. Brought for judgement before her father her identity was confirmed and he was converted together with her mother. Both she and her mother were martyred in Rome; her father became a bishop and was also martyred. Feast: December 25.

Eulalia (d. c.304) This 12-year-old Spanish girl was tortured and burned alive at Merida for refusing to sacrifice to pagan gods. Feast: December 10.

Another Eulalia, said to have been martyred at Barcelona, is possibly one and the same person but has a different feast day on February 12.

Eustace (d. c.118) Originally, he is said to have been a Roman captain of the Imperial Guard, called Placidas, whose family were converted to Christianity after a stag, with a crucifix between its horns, appeared to him while he was out hunting. He adopted the name Eustace and, on losing his fortune, fled with his family to Egypt. He became separated from his wife who fell into the hands of pirates, while his sons were taken by a wolf and a lion. After many years of farm labour, he was recalled to Rome and the Guard and was reunited with his family, all of whom had managed to escape their fates. When they refused to offer pagan sacrifice, they were all martyred by being roasted inside a brass bull. Feast: September 20 (until 1969); November 2 in the East.

F

Fabian (d. 250) He was elected pope in 236, although a layman, allegedly because a dove settled on his head, presumably as a sign of his holiness. He was martyred early on during the Decian persecution. Feast: January 20.

Fabiola (d. 399) A Roman patrician of the celebrated Fabia family and follower of St Jerome, she divorced her husband because of his debauchery. Widowed following the death of her second husband, she took up charitable works, aiding churches, and built the first Christian public hospital in the West. Feast: December 27.

Faith or Foy (3rd century) A Gallic martyr, legend says she was roasted on a metal grill before being beheaded at Agen. Feast: October 6. *See* Sophia.

Felicity (d. c.165) This Roman matron allegedly bore seven sons, all of whom were martyred on the orders of Emperor Antonius Pius. She was beheaded, as were Alexander, Vitalis and Martial; Silvanus was drowned in the Tiber, Januarius scourged until he died while Felix and Philip were clubbed to death. The bodies of these so-called Seven Brothers were found to have been buried in close proximity to Felicity and this may have given the false impression that they were her sons. Feast: July 10.

Felix (d c.304) He was a Roman priest who, on his way to execution during Diocletian's persecution, was joined by an unknown stranger who, also professing Christianity, chose to die with him. He is forever linked to Felix and known as Adauctus (the added one). Their joint feast day is August 30.

There are many other saints called Felix including more than 60 martyrs. One of them was a bishop of Thibiuca who was beheaded at Carthage for refusing to surrender Christian Scriptures for burning. He died on July 15 but another version of the story which says that he was taken to Italy for execution led to his feast being celebrated on October 24.

Fiacre (d. c.670) An Irishman, he decided to build an hospice for travellers in France near his hermitage at Breuil in Brie where the bishop of Meaux offered him as much land as he could dig in one day. Many visited him hoping for cures as well as spiritual guidance. He is patron saint of gardeners, sufferers from venereal disease and Paris cab drivers. The name 'fiacre' was later given to the carriages which plied their trade outside the Hôtel Saint-Fiacre. Feast: September 1.

Finbar (c.560-c.623) His baptismal name was Lochan but the monks who educated him called him Fionnbharr (white head). A hermit who attracted many disciples, he was a founder of monasteries, the most important being in Cork, Ireland. The town developed around the monastery and he later became bishop and patron saint of that city. Feast: September 25.

Finnian (d. 549) This Irish monk founded several monasteries, the most important being that at Clonard where he became abbot and attracted many disciples to his teaching. His monasticism had a strong Welsh influence as he had pursued his studies in Wales in earlier times. He died of plague, according to one hagiographer 'for the sake of the people of the Gael, that they might not all perish of the yellow pest'. Feast: December 12.

Finnian of Moville (d. 579) After studying in Ireland and Scotland he became a monk at Ninian's monastery of Whithorn which, it is said, he was forced to leave because of a joke at the expense of a Pictish princess who was in love with him. Ordained in Rome, he founded monasteries on his return to Ireland of which Moville in County Down was the most important. He was the tutor of St Columba and became involved in a dispute with him when he made a copy of the psalter of St Jerome which Finnian had brought from Rome. Finian insisted that he should have the copy and King Dairmaid ruled that Columba hand it over to him. Miracles attributed to him include moving the position of a river. Feast: September 10.

Flavian (d. 449) A patriarch of the church at Constantinople, he offended

the Emperor Theodosius III by refusing to send expensive presents to his coronation or to make his sister a deaconess. He was involved in a conflict with the local abbot who denied that Christ had two natures after the Incarnation – the beginnings of monophysitism. This led to Flavian being deposed and at the unruly Council of Ephesus he was assaulted so severely that he died three days later. Feast: February 18.

Also a Syrian monk (d. 512) who was created patriarch of Antioch in 482 and who was also deposed for his opposition to monophysitism. He died in exile in Petra. Feast: July 20.

Florian (d. 304) A Roman army officer in Austria during the persecution of Diocletion, he declared himself a Christian and was scourged and thrown into the River Enns with a weight around his neck. Patron of Poland. Feast: May 4.

Francis of Assisi (1181-1226) The sybaritic son of a cloth-merchant who, after capture and imprisonment during a war with Perugia, became seriously ill. During this time he received powerful visions in which he was urged to help the poor and sick. This he did, even exchanging his own rich clothes for those of a former

The Martyrdom of St Florian *by Albrecht Altdorfer (c.1480-1538).*

acquaintance reduced to beggary. A voice appearing to come from the crucifix on the altar of the dilapidated church of San Damiano instructed Francis to repair it so, taking a horse and loading it with merchandise belonging to his father, he set out to sell it, donating the proceeds to the church. His outraged father considered him mad and even chained him up. Eventually, disowned and disinherited, he embarked on a religious life, sacrificing even the clothes he stood up in. After years spent as a wandering mendicant, he returned to San Damiano where he persuaded the townsfolk to give alms and assistance to rebuild it. He also repaired another church and the chapel of St Mary of the Angels, living close by and attracting a group of disciples, among them St Clare (q.v.). In 1210, Pope Innocent III approved the establishment of the Order of Friars Minor, whose Rule stressed poverty and an intense spiritual life (though, after 300 years of contention between the more austere and the less strict friars the latter formally broke away to form the Friars Minor Conventual, or Black Friars, with some relaxation of the need for strict poverty and with property held in common). Preachers and missionaries, they taught by their own example. In the next few years, Francis set out to convert the Moslems but shipwreck and illness prevented him from reaching Syria and Morocco, though he did reach Egypt. There he denounced the immorality and greed of the crusaders laying siege to Damietta and passed through Muslim lines to meet the Sultan Malek al-Kamil, by whom he was kindly received. However, his arguments made no converts and a proposed ordeal of walking through fire, as a confirmation of the True Faith, was rejected by the Imams. Francis, more than any other saint, is associated with nature. He is said to have preached to the birds, who listened carefully then flew away in

the shape of a cross: he tamed a wolf that was terrorizing the town of Gubbio by supposedly making it sign a treaty which he dictated to it. In 1223, at Grecchio, he made a Christmas crib with ox and ass standing by which, if not the first, established this as a popular world-wide custom. The following year, while praying in his cell on Mount Alverna that he might take upon himself the agony of Christ on the Cross, he had a vision in which he received the stigmata, marks on hands and feet duplicating the wounds of crucifixion. Thereafter, his life consisted of suffering and declining health but also of spiritual happiness. In 1225, he wrote the beautiful *Canticle of the Sun* when making a last visit to St Clare. He died at Assisi and was buried first in the church of San Giorgio and later moved in 1230 to the new basilica built by Elias to contain his relics. Feast: October 4.

Francis of Nagasaki (d. 1597)
A doctor from Miako, he was converted by Franciscan missionaries and became a tertiary friar (one who follows Franciscan ideals while remaining a layman). Christian missionaries were being expelled from Japan in 1587 but some stayed, pretending to be traders. A sea-captain's boast that the role of the priests was to make it easier for the Portuguese or Spaniards to conquer led to the arrest and execution of 26 Christians: three Jesuits, six Franciscan priests (Spaniards, a Spanish Mexican and one from India) the remainder being tertiaries who were all Japanese, except for Francis, and ranged from the high-born Paul Miki to three teenage boys. Though there were more to follow, these first Japanese martyrs had their ears mutilated and were paraded streaked with blood as a warning to others. They were then

lashed and chained to crosses which were raised in a row. Individual executioners with lances killed them simultaneously.
Feast: February 6.

Francis of Paola (c.1416-1507)
Founder of the Minim Friars, this Calabrian boy was educated by Franciscans, becoming a hermit near Paola at the age of 15. Here, with two others, he developed a community which was to grow into the order of Minim Friars. The monastery at Paola was followed by other foundations, including several in France (where he was sent at the request of the dying Louis XI), Spain and Germany. He gained a reputation for prophecy and miracles and died at the monastery built for him at Plessis by Charles VIII. His Order, which added abstinence from meat to the Franciscan vows, was approved by Sixtus IV in 1474, being known at

first as the Hermits of St Francis of
Assisi. Feast: April 2.

Francis of Sales (1567-1622)
Destined to become bishop of Geneva
and a Doctor of the Church, he
became a monk when only 9 years
old. Only after he had gained a
Doctorate of Law at Padua in 1591
did he admit to his father, a Savoy
aristocrat, that he intended to pursue
a life in the Church. He was
ordained in 1593 and appointed
provost of Geneva becoming deeply
engaged in missionary work designed
to win protestants back to Rome.
Travelling through Chablais, preaching
and writing tracts, he was not only
in danger from Calvinists, but was
trapped up a tree all night surrounded
by wolves. After strict examination
in theology in Rome he was
appointed coadjutor of Geneva
in 1599 and bishop in 1602. His
Treatise on the Love of God, which
stresses that sanctity can be part of
everyday life, and *Introduction to a
Devout Life*, written as instruction for
a lay cousin, are his best known
writings. Patron of journalists.
Feast: January 24.

Francis Xavier (1506-1551)
Born into the Basque nobility, he
met Ignatius de Loyola while studying
in Paris and in 1534 became one of the
first seven Jesuits to take their vows.
Appointed apostolic nuncio to the
Indies, he worked in Goa in southern
India (which he made his
headquarters), the spice islands of
Indonesia, and the Philippines.
He set out for China but died, on an
island in the Canton River,
accompanied only by a Chinese boy
called Antony, without setting foot on
the mainland. He was a fervent
preacher, though communicating
through interpreters, and gained the
confidence of the poor by eating the
same food as them and sleeping on the
ground. His prolific correspondence
gives a vivid insight into his missionary
methods. Feast: December 3.

G

Gabriel, The Archangel Messenger
of God. He appeared to Mary
announcing to her that she had been
chosen to be the Mother of God. One
of the few angels to be given a name in
biblical texts he appears in the writings
of all the great religions. He also
announced the birth of John the
Baptist to Elizabeth when she had long
given up hope of childbearing. Feast:
formerly March 24, since 1969
September 29, March 26 in the East.

Gabriel Lalement (1610-1649)
Jesuit martyr. Feast: October 19. *See*
Isaac Jogues.

Gall (d. c.635)
Was a missionary to
Gaul and then to the area near Lake
Zürich and Bregenz in Austria before
settling as a hermit and preacher where
the Benedictine abbey and town

named after him later developed. Feast:
October 16.

Genesius (3rd century)
An actor
who, performing in a satire on
Christians and about to be 'baptized',
underwent a real conversion. Presented
to Emperor Diocletian after the
performance he declared his faith, was
tortured when he refused to sacrifice to
pagan gods and was beheaded. Patron
saint of actors. Feast: August 25.

Also a notary (d. c.303) of Arles
in Provence, he chose to quit his post
rather than record a decree of
Diocletian and Maximiam persecuting
Christians. He fled, was refused
baptism by a bishop who feared
betrayal and was caught and beheaded.
Feast: June 3.

Genevieve (c.422-500)
Dedicating
herself to God at the age of 7, after a

meeting with St Germain at Nanterre, the orphaned girl went to Paris and at 15 became a nun when she began to have visions and make prophecies. When the Franks besieged Paris she led a party to bring in provisions by river, obtaining the release of prisoners from the conquering Childeric and Clovis (who gave her their respect) and prophesized that prayer and fasting would spare the city from Attila and his Huns, who did in fact take a different route. She was instrumental in building a church in honour of St Denis and in Clovis's building of SS Peter and Paul, later named after her, where she was buried and where many miracles were attributed to her. (Rebuilt, then secularized, it is now the Panthéon). When she went to pray it was said she could miraculously light a candle without fire or flint and when the devil tried to blow it out an angel always kept it lit. Patron of Paris. Feast: January 3.

George (d. c.303) Possibly a centurion in the Roman army who was martyred at Lydda, near modern Tel Aviv, he was supposedly dragged along the ground by horses, then roasted in a brass bull before being beheaded. Legend says that he came to a city terrorized by a dragon to which its citizens daily sacrificed a maiden – this day the king's daughter. He overcame the dragon, made the maiden's girdle into a harness and bade her lead it into the city where he converted the citizens before finally killing the dragon. Patron of England, Portugal, Greece, Catalonia, Venice and Genoa and of soldiers he is invoked against plague, leprosy and venereal disease. Feast: April 23, demoted in 1969 to local celebration; April 18 in the Coptic Church.

Other **SS George** include a hermit on Mount Olympus (martyred c.730), February 12; two monks who became bishop of Antioch and bishop of Mitylene who opposed iconoclasm (d. 814 and 816), April 19 and April 7; a monk who became bishop of

SANCTA GENOVEFA

Amastris and defended his city against Saracens (d. 825); and a Georgian abbot of Iviron on Mount Athos who translated Greek religious texts into the Georgian (1014-1066), June 30.

Germain or Germanus (c.496-576)

He was the austere abbot of Saint-Symphorien in Autun before going to Paris where he was an outspoken critic of court morals. He went so far as to excommunicate Childebert I, a king whom he had miraculously cured of a fatal illness. He was twice sent to Britain to refute Pelagianism. He founded the church and monastery in Paris later renamed after him as Saint-Germain-des-Prés. Feast: May 28.

Gertrude (the Great) (d. 1302)

Educated in a Benedictine monastery at Helfta in Saxony from the age of 5, she became a nun at 26 after experiencing the first of many visions of Christ which she described in her *Revelations*. Patron of the West Indies. Feast: November 16.

Gertrude of Nivelles (626-659)

Was the first abbess of the monastery built by her saintly parents and celebrated for its hospitality. Patron of travellers and gardeners. Feast: March 17.

Gervase and Protase (1st or 2nd century)

These twin brothers were only children when they were martyred in Milan, Gervase being beaten with a lead-tipped scourge and his brother either beaten with a whip or beheaded. Another version of the story says that they were the children of St Vitalis who, after their parents'execution, lived as hermits until, refusing army service, they were martyred. Feast: June 19.

Giles (d. c.710)

Founder of the monastery that later bore his name on land provided by King Wamba, he was probably a genuine hermit and lived near the mouth of the Rhône.

Many legends are told of him, the chief among them being that he was an Athenian who fled to Provence to escape the attention generated by a miracle he had performed; in another, a deer fed him with her milk and sought his protection when hunted by Wamba whose arrows crippled Giles instead. Wamba (in some accounts it is Charlemagne) sought absolution for a sin which he dared not confess. Giles saw what it was, written on a list shown to him by an angel. As he interceded on the king's behalf, the words disappeared and the king admitted his sin and repented. This led to Giles' veneration by all loath to make a spoken confession. Patron of cripples, lepers, nursing mothers and blacksmiths. Feast: September 1.

Gregory the Great (c.540-604)

This Roman patrician and prefect of the city gave away his possessions and turned his home into a monastery where he became a monk. Called to serve the Church in administrative and diplomatic roles for several years, he returned to his monastery as abbot and planned to lead a group of missionaries to Britain thus earning the title 'Apostle of the English'. According to the Venerable Bede, he had seen Anglo-Saxon slaves in a market place in Britain and declared them to be 'not Angles but angels'. In the interim, however, he was elected pope and sent Augustine on the mission in his place. He resisted the power of Byzantium and exercised temporal power in Italy, reinforcing the supremacy of papal authority. He insisted on clerical celibacy, played an important part in the development of the liturgy and founded monasteries and choir schools where the famous Chant bearing his name was taught. Reported miracles include the appearance of Christ as an extra guest at a supper he gave for 12 paupers and, when the Empress Constantia declared a shroud of

John the Evangelist, which he presented to her to be a fake, he cut it with a knife causing it to bleed. Feast: September 3.

Three further popes are among the many other SS Gregory.

Grimbald or Grimwald (c.825-901)

This Flemish monk and eminent scholar was first invited to England by Alfred the Great in order to help him with religious translations into English. He declined the archbishopric of Canterbury, accepting instead the deanship of Winchester's New Minster. He is regarded as the founder of Oxford University. Feast: July 8.

H

Harlampius (d. c.202)

A priest of Asia Minor, his name means 'shining with joy' (because of his Faith). He is said to have lived and died in the town of Magnesia, though this is uncertain. For refusing to sacrifice to Roman gods, he was sentenced to be flayed alive before the Emperor (either Severus or Lucian) who, being impatient of the torturer's slowness, seized the knife himself but was unable to touch the saint. Instead, his own hands were cut off, which Harlampius miraculously restored. This did not, however, prevent him from being eventually beheaded. February 10, in the East only.

Helena (c.250-330)

The mother of Constantine the Great, she was of lowly birth, probably the daughter of a Bithynian inn-keeper who married a Roman general. When he became Caesar, however, he divorced her in order to marry Maximian's stepdaughter. Originally anti-Christian, she was over 60 when, after the visionary experience and victory of her son the Emperor Constantine (q.v.), she was converted. With him, she founded many churches and on a pilgrimage to the Holy Land was guided by a vision and discovered the True Cross, the

marble steps climbed by Jesus on the way to His judgement by Pilate (taken to Rome and now the *Scala Sancta* of the Lateran palace), a seamless robe worn by Jesus at the Crucifixion and the nails with were used to crucify Him. Feast: August 18

Helier (6th century) Originally from Tongres, Belgium, he was raised by a Christian priest who was murdered by his pagan father. He came to live as a hermit in a cave on the island of Jersey where the town, which later bore his name, developed.

40

He was murdered by brigands whom he was attempting to convert. Feast: July 16.

Henry of Finland (d. c.1156) An Englishman, he appears to have been part of the household of Nicholas Breakspear and so accompanied him to Scandinavia in 1151 when the cardinal (later Pope Adrian IV) was papal legate. There, he was made bishop of Uppsala and accompanied Eric of Sweden on a campaign to Finland, remaining there to convert the defeated Finns. Later, one of these

converts whom he excommunicated for murder, attacked and killed him with an axe. Patron of Finland. Feast: January 19.

Hervé or Harvey (6th century) The blind child of a British bard in Brittany, he was first a teacher and then abbot at Plouvien, later founding a new monastery at Lanhouarneau. Miracles attributed to him include the story of a wolf which ate a donkey while it was ploughing a field. At the command of the saint the wolf leaped into the

traces and finished the task itself. Feast: June 17

Hilarion (c.291-c.371) A Palestinian from Gaza, he was baptized at the age of 15 when he visited St Antony in the desert. On his return, and finding his parents dead, he gave everything to the poor and became a hermit, living for many years on a diet of 15 figs a day. His life of austerity and the miracles attributed to him attracted unwelcome attention and, when he was in his sixties, he moved on, first to St Antony's Egyptian hermitage (after a

LEFT
The Temptation of St Hilarion *by Dominique Louis Papéty (1815-1849). Like St Antony and other hermits he was subjected to temptations of the flesh.*

FAR LEFT
St Helena and Heraclius taking the Holy Cross to Jerusalem *by Martin Bernat (1454-1497) and Miguel Jimenez (dates unknown).*

were written down by a scribe as *Scivias*. She also wrote on medicine and natural history, composed poems, hymns, a morality play and wrote to many rulers and churchmen admonishing them to adopt better conduct. Feast: September 17.

Hippolytus (d. c.235) Priest and author of refutations of heresies, he was elected anti-pope in opposition to Callixtus whom he considered to be too lenient towards heretics. He was exiled to Sardinia during the persecution of Maximinus where he was martyred or died from his privations. Another tradition holds that he was the jailor and convert of St Laurence and was torn apart by horses near the mouth of the Tiber (Hippolytus means unleashed horse). This tale was possibly told due to confusion with another martyr of the same name. Patron of horses. August 13.

Hope *See* Sophia.

Hubert (d. 727) An evangelist of the Ardennes, bishop of Maastricht and, after transferral of the see, of Liege. He is connected to a 14th-century legend, similar to that of St Eustace, in which he is said to have seen a crucifix between the horns of a stag when hunting on Good Friday. This was presumably the reason for his attraction to the religious life. Patron of huntsmen. Feast: November 3.

revelation of the hermit's death) and then to Sicily, Dalmatia and Cyprus, seeking solitude and anonymity even though reported miracles continued to draw attention to him.
Feast: October 21.

Hilary (d. c.368) A married man when converted, he became bishop of Poitiers but was condemned and exiled for opposing Arianism, returning to Gaul in 360. Author of many theological treatises he is one of the Doctors of the Church.
Feast: January 13.

Also a nobleman from Lorraine (c.400-449) who gave his possessions away on conversion and joined a monastery. He was bishop of Arles from 429 where he was noted for his oratory. Feast: May 5

Other **SS Hilary** include a pope (d. 468), February 28; and a Tuscan hermit (d. 558), May 15.

Hilda (614-680) A member of a Northumbrian royal family, she converted to Christianity at the age of 13, became a nun at 33 and was later abbess at Hartlepool and founder or refounder of Whitby in 657, making it a centre of learning and education. She gave encouragement to the poet Caedmon and both rulers and the general populace came to her for advice. Feast: November 17.

Hildegard of Bingen (1098-1179) A sickly child, she was placed in the care of a noblewoman and hermit at the age of eight, becoming a nun and eventually prioress of the Benedictine community that developed around the hermitage. In mid-life she began to have visions and revelations which

Hugh of Lincoln (c.1140-1200) Born in Avalon, in imperial Burgundy, he was a monk at Villarbenoît before joining the order of the Grande Chartreuse. He was invited by Henry II of England to become prior of Charterhouse at Witham in Somerset (which the king founded in reparation for the murder of Thomas Becket), and was later created bishop of Lincoln. A fearless critic of the monarchy, he supported the common people against oppressive forest laws, personally tended lepers, risked his own life in attempts to

protect Jews during anti-semitic riots, and made Lincoln a major centre of learning. Feast: November 17.

Also Little St Hugh (d. 1255), a nine-year old whose body was discovered hidden in a well. He was rumoured to have been ritually murdered by Lincoln Jews who, trying to bury the body found that the ground would not accept it. The story, however, reflects local envy of wealthy local Jews which was current at the time and has no basis in fact.
Feast: August 27.

Other **SS Hugh** include an abbot of Cluny (1024-1109), a reformist adviser to the papacy, April 29; and a bishop of Grenoble (1052-1132) whose support and gift of land helped establish the Carthusian Order. April 1.

Humphrey (d. 871) French monk and bishop of Thérouanne from 856, he fled when Norsemen sacked and burned the city and played an important part in its reconstruction and the rebuilding of the St-Bertin monastery at Saint-Omer, of which he also became the abbot.
Feast: March 8.

Hyacinth (1185-1257) A nephew of a bishop of Cracow who appointed him a canon and took him to Rome where he met Dominic and became a member of his Order. He evangelized Poland and beyond, spreading the gospel to Scandinavia and Russia. He founded

Dominican houses in Poland which sent out missionaries and he is credited with numerous miracles. Feast: August 17.

Also a chamberlain (d. c.120) of the Emperor Trajan who was imprisoned and scourged for being a Christian. He refused to eat meat consecrated to pagan gods and died of starvation. Feast: July 3.

Also a martyred slave (4th century), beheaded with his brother Protus, September 11.

I

Ida (d. 825) A granddaughter of Charlemagne and raised in his court, she was widowed young and thereafter devoted her life to the poor, founding a convent at Herzfeld where she died. Feast: September 4.

Ignatius of Antioch (d. c.107) He was bishop of Antioch when sentenced to death in the arena during the persecution of Trajan. The ship taking him to Rome hugged the coast and Ignatius was received with honour by Christians at each port of call where he wrote seven letters to various communities containing instruction on marriage and Christian ideology. He was eaten by lions in the Colosseum in Rome. Feast: October 17.

Ignatius of Loyola (1491-1556) Founder of the Jesuits, he was the youngest child of a Basque nobleman. While recovering from wounds received at the battle of Pamplona he began to study the lives of Christ and the Saints and decided to devote himself to God. After a pilgrimage to Monserrat and a year spent in retreat, during which he experienced visions and wrote his *Spiritual Exercises*, he spent ten years in teaching and study before forming the Society of Jesus with Francis Xavier and other students in Paris. Prevented from carrying out their plans to visit Jerusalem, they went to Rome to offer their service to the pope (Ignatius had already had a vision of Christ carrying a heavy cross saying 'I will be favourable to you in Rome'). The Society was

formally established as a religious Order, its members taking their vows in 1541, and he passed the rest of his life in Rome as its Superior General. Patron of retreats and spiritual exercises. Feast: July 31.

Illtyd (450-535) According to legend, he originated either in Brittany or Britain, visited King Arthur, married Trynihid and served under a Welsh chieftain before he and his wife continued life as recluses, eventually founding a monastery for the disciples he attracted at Llanillltud Fawr (Llantwit) in Glamorgan. Other versions say he was a learned disciple of St Germain, was head of the school at Llantwit and even identify him with the Arthurian Sir Galahad.
Feast: November 6

Innocent (d. c.350) A Christian of Tortona in northern Italy, he was arrested there but escaped and fled to Rome where he became a deacon returning to Tortona as bishop in 322. Feast: April 17.

Other **SS Innocent** include popes Innocent I (d. 417) a strong proponent of papal supremacy, July 28; Innocent V (1225-1276); The Blessed Innocent XI (1611-1689) was beatified in 1956.

Irenaeus (c.130-200) Possibly from Smyrna and a pupil of Polycarp, he became a priest and later a bishop of Lyons. An evangelist in Gaul and peacemaker between different factions of the Church, he was an important theologian, especially in his refutation of Gnosticism. Often venerated as a martyr, there is no firm evidence of martyrdom. Feast: June 28, August 23 in the East.

Other **SS Iranaeus** – all martyrs – include Iranaeus (d. 304) beheaded at Sirmium (near modern Mitrovica in Yugoslavia), March 24; and a deacon (d. 273) imprisoned and tortured after burying another martyr at Chiusi, Italy. He received further torture and died when visited by Mustiola, a Christian woman, who spurned the local

magistrate's advances. She was then clubbed to death. July 3.

Irene (d. 304) Sister of Agape (q.v.). Feast: April 3. *See also* Sebastian for another St Irene.

Isaac (d. 439) He became a monk when his wife died and became Patriarch (Catholicos) of Armenia, as did his father before him, in 390. He gained independence for the Armenian church, reforming and developing it and promoted the creation of an Armenian alphabet and the translation of the Bible and other works. Feast: September 9.

Isaac Jogues (1607-1646) A Jesuit missionary from Orléans, he was sent to French Canada to convert the Mohawks. Captured by Iroquois on a medical mission to the Hurons with surgeon René Goupil (who was executed), he escaped and returned to France. Sent back, the Iroquois blamed a box of his religious objects for crop failures and an epidemic and he and his lay assistant, Jean Lalande from Dieppe, were seized. He was attacked with tomahawks and beheaded, while Lalande was executed the next day. Two years later, Anthony Daniel was killed by Iroquois attacking a Huron village where he had just celebrated Mass, and the following year, 1649, Jean de Brébeuf of Normandy, and Gabriel Lalement, from Paris, were captured in an Iroquois attack, tortured and killed. A few months later the same fate befell Charles Garnier, from Paris, who was killed in another attack while attempting to minister to the dying; his companion, Noel Chabanel, from Mende, was murdered as he returned to the village. These men were canonized together in 1930 as Martyrs of North America and share the same feast day of October 19.

Isidore (c.560-636) Born in Seville of a noble Cartegenian family, he became bishop of Seville, completed the conversion of the Visigoths from Arianism and reorganized the Church

in Spain. His presidency of Church Councils at Seville and Toledo resulted in a decree that cathedral schools be established in every diocese. A Doctor of the Church, he was famed for his learning and his encyclopedic writing which ranged from astronomy and geography to history and theology. Feast: April 4.

Other **SS Isidore** include three Egyptians: a soldier martyr from Alexandria (d. c.251) who was denounced as a Christian and beheaded on Chios, May 15; a wealthy follower of St Athanasius (319-404) who gave away his wealth to become a hermit and was later a director of a hospital in Constantinople, January 15; and another Alexandrian who became abbot of Lychnos and famous for thousands of letters of theological instruction and exhortation. Feast: February 4.

Isidore the Farmer (c.1080-1130)
After the death of their child, he and his wife, St Maria de la Cabeza, lived a continent and devout life. Legends tell how his employer saw a team of white oxen, driven by angels, ploughing alongside Isidore's team. Another time, on a winter's day, he poured out half a sack of grain to feed a flock of hungry-looking birds to the jeers to his companions. When they returned to the mill, the sack was full again and when milled produced twice its volume of flour. Patron of farmers and of Madrid. Feast: May 15.

Ives or Ia (date unknown) Legend describes her as a virgin who sailed across the Irish Sea on a leaf. Patron of St Ives, in Cornwall. Feast: February 3.

Also a Persian bishop who came to Britain and became a hermit at Slepe, now St Ives in what was once Huntingdonshire. Feast: October 27.

J

James the Great (d. 44) The son of Zebedee, he became a fisherman and later, with his brother John, a disciple of Jesus in Galilee and was the first of the apostles to be martyred, beheaded in Jerusalem. Though buried there, legend describes the removal of his body to Spain, where he is said to have travelled as a missionary, and the erection of a shrine which was discovered in the 9th century. The great church of Santiago de Compostela was erected on the spot and has become almost as great a centre of pilgrimage as Rome. Patron

St Jerome and the Lion *by Vittore Carpaccio (c.1460/5–1523/6).*

of Spain, his symbol is the scallop shell – hence the name of the dish *Coquilles Saint-Jacques*. Feast: July 25.

James the Less (d. 62) Little is known of him but he may have been a cousin of Jesus or his half-brother by a previous wife of Joseph. He was one of the apostles and became head of the Church in Jerusalem. He was arraigned by the Sanhedrin and sentenced to stoning but some say that he was thrown from the walls of the Temple into the valley of Jehosophat and there clubbed to death. Feast: May 3.

Januarius or Gennaro (d. c.305) Originating from Naples or Benevento, of which town he was made bishop, he and his deacon Festus (or Faustus) were arrested during the persecution of Diocletian at Pozzuoli when visiting imprisoned Christians and were thrown to

to wild beasts in Apamea after preaching the Gospel there. Feast: July 12.

Jean de Brébeuf (1593-1649) Jesuit martyr. Feast: October 19. *See* Isaac Jogues.

Jean Lalande (d. 1646) Jesuit martyr. Feast: October 19. *See* Isaac Jogues.

Jeremy or Elias (d. 309) An Egyptian who with companions Daniel, Isaias and Samuel went to succour Christians condemned to the Cilician salt mines under the persecution of Maximus and were caught, tortured and beheaded. Feast: February 16.

Jerome or Hieronymus (c. 342-420) One of the principal Doctors of the Church, he was born at Strido, near Aquileia, in Dalmatia, and was highly educated by his father and in Rome before his baptism at 19 – though his devotion to religion seems to have begun in Trier. For a time he settled in Aquileia but conflict with other scholars sent him on a pilgrimage to Jerusalem. When he reached Antioch he had a vision in which he was whipped by angels who accused him of caring more for Latin and the classics than for the language of the bible. He decided, therefore, to study Hebrew and live as a hermit in the Syrian desert. Here, he was tempted by visions of sensuous women. He returned to Antioch, where he was ordained, and studied further in Constantinople and Rome where he became secretary to Pope Damasus, beginning the revision of the Gospels and other Scriptures. After the pope's death, he continued this work which culminated in the Vulgate Bible. In Bethlehem, he lived in a cell cut from the rock and linked to a monastery which he had established, helped by devout women who had become his followers in Rome. Legend tells of a lion which appeared, terrifying the monks. Jerome saw that it was limping and removed a thorn lodged in its paw and the grateful lion stayed in his

service. When travelling merchants stole the monastery's ass, the lion was at first accused of eating it, but it followed the thieves, scared them off and rescued the ass. Feast: September 30.

Joachim (1st century) According to the apocryphal *Gospel of James* he was the wealthy husband of St Anne and father of the Virgin Mary. Though he was a devout man, the Temple refused his offerings because they thought his lack of children was a punishment for a past sin. So he retreated to a hut in the wilderness for 40 days and nights when he was visited by an angel who told him to return to his wife. The child that was born was without taint of Original Sin. She was destined to become the Mother of God and was later known as The Immaculate Conception. Feast: July 26.

Joan of Arc (1412-1431) This peasant girl from Domrémy, Champagne, saw a blinding light and heard voices, later identified as those of SS Michael, Catherine and Margaret, which told her that she must save France from the conquering English. Her accurate prediction of further defeats eventually caused the local commander to take her seriously and she was sent to the king at Chinon. Here she was able to identify the king, even though he was disguised, and, by means of a secret sign given by her voices, convinced him she was genuine. After examination by theologians at Poitiers, she was allowed to take to the field of battle with a small force and went to the relief of besieged Orléans and pressed on to Rheims where she saw Charles VII crowned. She was wounded in an unsuccessful assault on Paris and after a winter of truce was captured by Burgundian forces while attempting to break a siege at Compiègne. They sold her to the English, who had her tried by the Inquisition for witchcraft and heresy. When she refused to recant, they burned her at the stake. A patron of France. Feast: May 30.

wild beasts. The beasts failed to harm them so they were beheaded instead. A vial of red substance, said to be his blood, is kept in the cathedral in Naples where it is said to miraculously liquify and bubble at certain times. Patron of Naples.
Feast: September 19.

Jason (1st century) Some say that St Paul stayed at his house in Salonika when on his second missionary journey and that he was a convert to Christianity. He may be the same person or confused with another Jason who was bishop of Tarsus and evangelized Corfu before being thrown

John the Apostle (1st century) He was a son of Zebedee and the brother of James the Great and together they fished the Sea of Galilee until called by Jesus to become his disciples. Though given prominence by Jesus, with James and Peter, little is known apart from what is contained in the Gospel stories. One tradition holds that he was martyred in Jerusalem at the same time as his brother; another claims that he was charged with the care of the Virgin Mary after the Crucifixion. He was also prominent in the early Church and went to Ephesus where he wrote the contemplative *Gospel of St John*. Although it could also be his work, claims that he is author of the *Book of Revelations* are difficult to substantiate for they are so different in style and content. However, later tradition, unquestioned until recent times, accepts him to be one and the same person as that visionary writer. After refusing to acknowledge the emperor Domitian as a god, he is said to have been immersed in a cauldron of boiling oil from which he emerged unscathed. Challenged to drink poison to prove the power of God, the poison is said to have climbed from the cup in the form of a snake, enabling him to

drink unharmed. Accused of being a magician, he was exiled to Patmos. Feast: December 27.

John of Avila (1499-1569) A wealthy Spaniard, he lived austerely and after his parents died gave his wealth to the poor. He was planning to go to Mexico but was persuaded to do missionary work in Andalucia instead. A powerful preacher and fearless critic of evil in high places, he was brought before the Inquisition accused of preaching that the rich could not get to heaven, but was, however, released. Writer of many sermons and letters on religious subjects, he was spiritual adviser to Teresa of Avila, St John of the Cross and others. Feast: May 10.

John Baptist de la Salle (1651-1719) Priest and educationalist from a noble family of Rheims, he helped instigate the opening of two schools for poor boys in that city, later inviting them to share his family home. He developed training schemes for teachers, reformatories for delinquent children and a religious teaching order, the Brothers of the Christian Schools, proposing that no brother could become a priest and no priest a

brother. His method replaced individual teaching in Latin with classes in the vernacular and on Sundays he offered technical teaching along with religious instruction. He insisted pupils be silent during lessons and was criticized by some for offering poor pupils education in more than manual skills and for severity to novice teachers. Patron of teachers. Feast: April 7 (formerly May 15).

John the Baptist (d. c.30) Regarded as a prophet in his lifetime, he was the son of Elizabeth and a Temple priest called Zacharius and a cousin of the Virgin Mary. An angel told his ageing mother that she would conceive and her son, John, both proclaimed the coming of the Messiah and baptized Him. He was a desert hermit and lived like an Old Testament prophet, subsisting on a diet of locusts and honey, preaching repentance and baptizing people in the river Jordan. Imprisoned for denouncing the incestuous union of Herod Antipas to Herodias (wife of his half-brother), he was beheaded when her daughter Salome demanded his head, this being the prize she exacted for agreeing to dance before the king. Feast: June 24

OPPOSITE

Joan of Arc *by Annie Louise Swynnerton (1844-1933)*

ABOVE

Altarpiece of The Virgin Mary attended by SS Catherine of Alexandria, John the Baptist, John the Evangelist and Barbara by Hans Memling (c.1440-1494). The left panel shows the execution of Saint John the Baptist, the right, Saint John the Evangelist on Patmos with his vision of the Apocalypse. The Baptist is one of the easiest saints to identify for he is usually shown in rough clothing, often with a wooden cross and holding or accompanied by a lamb in token of his proclamation 'the Lamb of God who takes away the sins of the world'. Catherine is identified by the wheel on which she was tortured and the sword with which she was executed. The infant Jesus, seated on His mother's lap, places a ring upon Catherine's finger. The Virgin Mary is said to have appeared to a hermit and bade him inform Catherine that she would be 'the bride of Christ'. He showed her a picture of the Madonna and Child and she was moved to love Christ and henceforth considered herself joined with him, as nuns are, in a mystic marriage. The Evangelist is identified by his cup of poison, Barbara by the tower beside her in which the Host (another of her attributes) is seen. Further episodes of the lives of the saints are shown between the columns and their capitals and in the background of the left panel.

(August 29 is a separate festival dedicated to his beheading).

John Chrysostom (c.347-407) A future Doctor of the Church, this soldier's son, born in Antioch, studied law and theology there before becoming a hermit. An austere life in a damp cave caused him to become seriously ill and he was forced to return to the city where he became a deacon and then a priest. His powerful preaching earned him the sobriquet Chrysostom (honey/golden-mouthed). Reluctantly, he accepted the post of Patriarch of Constantinople and set about the reform of the Church, abolishing unnecessary pomp and ostentation and spending all money saved on the poor. His criticism of public morals, vanity and extravagance made the Empress Eudoxia and even church colleagues his enemies and charges were brought against him for which he was deposed and exiled. An earthquake was taken as a sign of

divine disapproval of their action and the banishment cancelled, but it was carried out the following year when he was exiled to Pontus at the furthest end of the Black Sea. He died on the way there. Some of his letters and treatises survive and the Greek Orthodox Liturgy of St Chrysostom is attributed to him, though it was probably

composed after his death. Feast: September 13 in the West, November 13 in the East.

John of the Cross (1524-1591) A poor, though well-born Spaniard, he was an inept apprentice silk weaver and a servant in a hospital at Medina before becoming a Carmelite in 1563. He was planning to join the Carthusians when Teresa of Avila (q.v.) began to involve him in her reform of the Carmelites and establishment of the Discalced friars, first at Duruelo, then as rector of Alcala and later as confessor to the nuns of Avila. Opposition from the Calced Carmelites led to his imprisonment in Toledo and a savage public beating. After nine months he escaped and, in 1579, the two groups were given separate status. John founded a college at Baeza and other houses of his Order, becoming prior at Granada, then at Segovia. But new controversy saw him deprived of office and installed as a simple monk at remote La Penuela. Becoming ill, he was sent for treatment to Ubeda priory, where he shortly died. His mystical poetry includes *The Dark Night of the Soul*, written in prison, and *The Living Flame of Love*; commentaries on his own work which explore the need for asceticism. Feast: December 14.

John the Evangelist *See* John the Apostle.

Joseph (1st century) Husband of Mary the Mother of Jesus, he was a descendant of King David, living in Nazareth, who travelled to Bethlehem with his pregnant wife for a census (of which there is no historic record to give a dating) so that Jesus came to be born there. Angels told him he must accept Mary's Child and flee into Egypt to escape Herod's massacre of the first-born. Patron of the Catholic Church, of fathers, carpenters and other manual workers and seekers of a happy death. Feast: March 19. May 1 is the feast of 'Joseph the Worker'.

Joseph of Arimathea (1st century) A member of the Sanhedrin, the Jewish council of Judea (though he did not vote with the other members for Jesus' death) he obtained permission from Pilate, after the Crucifixion, to bury His body, which he interred in a tomb he had prepared for himself. Medieval legend says he came as a missionary to Britain carrying with him the Holy Grail, the chalice used by Jesus at the Last Supper. He is said to have planted his staff into the ground, at the place where he built a church, where it rooted and burst into flower. This is the famous thorn tree of Glastonbury. Feast: July 31 in the East and formerly March 17 in West.

Joseph Mkasa (d. 1886) A Christian convert in charge of King Mwanga of Uganda's pages, he was beheaded after speaking out against the king's debaucheries and his murder of Protestant missionary James Hannington and his party. He was the first of several martyred by Mwanga. Feast: June 3. *See also* Charles Lwanga.

Jude or Thaddeus (1st century) Both these names are mentioned in the Gospels of Mark and Matthew as one or other of the twelve disciples of Jesus but are generally considered to be one and the same person. He may be the writer of the *Epistle of Jude* and refers to himself as the brother of James, usually interpreted as meaning James the Less. Legend says he preached with Simon in Persia and was clubbed to death there. Patron saint of hopeless cases. Feast: October 28.

Julia (5th century) A Carthaginian noblewoman who, legend tells, was captured and sold into slavery. She was crucified for refusing to take part in pagan sacrifice in Corsica. Another version says she was killed by Saracens in a later century. Patron of Corsica. Feast: May 22.

Julian (d. 230) A gout-ridden Alexandrian who was scourged and

burned. Feast: February 27.

Also A Cilician (d. 302) who was sewn into a sack full of poisonous snakes and cast into the sea, March 16; a Gaul (d. 304), a former Roman army officer, who was beheaded near Brioude and is patron of the Auvergne, August 28; a Palestinian (d. 309) who, receiving religious instruction before baptism, was caught venerating St Elias' body and was burned, February 17; a hermit (d. 377) who lived on the banks of the Euphrates who refuted Arianism, January 17; a bishop of Le Mans (4th century), January 27; an archbishop of Toledo (d. 690), March 8; and a possibly mythical figure known as the Hospitaller (date unknown) to whom a deer, upbraiding him for hunting her, foretold that he would murder his father and mother. This came about when his parents visited his castle in his absence and his wife installed them in their own room. Returning unexpectedly, he mistook them for his wife with an adulterous lover and killed them both. Seeing his terrible mistake, he abandoned the castle and with his wife lived in a cave by a dangerous river where they operated a free ferry for travellers. Once he rescued a dying leper, put him in his own bed, and in a vision was told that his sin had been forgiven him. February 12.

Juliana (d. c.305) Refusing to marry, despite scourging and torture, she was imprisoned and is said to have argued with the Devil who tried to make her change her mind and marry the man of her father's choice. She survived roasting and boiling in oil before being beheaded, probably at Cumae, near Naples. Feast: February 16.

Justin (c.100-165) A Greco-Roman philosopher, his surviving texts contain the earliest known record of Christian lay intellectual debate. Denounced to the authorities when teaching in Rome, he was beheaded with six colleagues in the reign of Marcus Aurelius. Feast: June 1.

Justina (c.300) A virgin martyr, probably in the Maximian persecutions, she is now patron of Padua. A 12th-century account of her life claimed she was baptized by the first bishop of Padua and before her martyrdom knelt and prayed for courage on a bridge across the Po, leaving the impression of her knees behind. Feast: October 7.

Also a daughter of a Seville potter (date unknown) who, with her sister Rufina, broke pots rather than supply them for use in pagan worship and destroyed a statue of Venus. They were either thrown to the lions or Justina was racked and Rufina strangled. Patrons of Seville, whose Giralda tower they are said to have protected from lightning in 1504. July 19. *See also* Cyprian and Justina.

OPPOSITE

St John the Baptist, woodcut by Albrecht Dürer (1471-1528).

ABOVE RIGHT

The Holy Family under an Apple Tree by Hans van Balen (dates unknown). Also in the picture are SS Zacharius and Elizabeth and their son John the Baptist.

K

Kenelm (d. c.812) Historically, Glastonbury was part of this Mercian prince's lands and he probably died fighting the Welsh during his father Kenwulf's reign. But, according to medieval legend, he succeeded him at the age of 7 and was murdered at the instigation of his sister Quendreda (who in history was an abbess in Kent) so that she could claim the throne. Feast: July 17.

Kenneth or Canice (c.525-600) Irish-born, he was an associate of St Columba, became a monk in Wales, travelled to Rome, preached in Ireland and Scotland, and founded monasteries including one at Aghaboe. Feast: October 11.

Kevin (d. c.618) Irish abbot and hermit of Glendalough, County Wicklow, where his disciples formed a monastery. Legends tell how he lived for a time on fish which an otter brought to him. In another tale, he stood with one arm outstretched and a blackbird laid an egg on his hand. He stood praying until the egg hatched out. Feast: June 3.

Kilian (d. c.689) This Irish monk, possibly already a bishop, was a missionary along the Rhine and Maine rivers, converting Gozbert, ruler of Warzburg, where he was made bishop. Legend says that when he castigated Gozbert on his unlawful marriage to his brother's widow and insisted that he put an end to it, the wife, Geilana, had him killed, together with his companion missionaries. Patron of Warzburg. Feast: July 8.

L

Laurence or Lawrence (d. 258) Deacon of Pope Sixtus II who was martyred a few days before him in Valerian's persecution, and was known for his care of the poor. Tradition holds that he was Spanish-born and that Sixtus predicted his execution would take place three days later. So he took the opportunity to sell Church possessions and give money in alms before his arrest. His death was possibly by beheading but a myth developed that he was placed on a grill over a slow fire and even asked his torturers to turn him over when one side was well broiled. Patron of deacons. Feast: August 10.

Other **SS Laurence** include a hermit of Subiaco (1190-1243) who, killing a man accidentally in his youth, wore chain-mail next to his skin as a penance, August 16; a Capuchin Franciscan linguist and diplomat (1559-1619) who rode with the German armies against the Turks, July 21 (formerly July 23); and a missionary with St Augustine who was his successor as archbishop of Canterbury (d. 619). According to an account by Bede, when the Anglo-Saxons began to relapse into paganism, he decided to return to Gaul, but on waking from a

dream in which St Peter punished him, found his body still bore the marks of a lashing: showing these to the new Saxon king helped effect his conversion. February 3.

Laurence O'Toole (1128-1180) Abbot of Glendalough, he was a reforming archbishop of Dublin at the time of the Irish revolt against King Dermot and invasion by English forces

under the Earl of Pembroke which led to the sack of Dublin in 1170. Thereafter, he was a frequent peace negotiator between the English and Irish kings. Feast: November 14.

Lazarus (1st century) Brother of Martha and Mary, he was raised from the dead by Jesus at Bethany. Tradition says that he was set adrift from Jaffa with his sisters and others

in a boat without oars or rudder but all landed safely in Cyprus where he became bishop of Kition (Lanarca). Another version say that he landed in Gaul, becoming bishop of Marseille and dying a martyr under Domitian's persecution. Feast: December 17.

Leander (c.550-600) A bishop and Doctor of the Spanish Church, he was the brother of Isidore, monk and

The Martyrdom of Saint Laurence *by Valentin de Boulogne (1594-1632).*

bishop of Seville from 584, opposed Arianism, reformed the Spanish liturgy and wrote a rule for nuns. Feast: February 27.

Leo the Great (d. 461) Destined to be a Doctor of the Church, he was possibly of Tuscan origin though born in Rome and was already an important Church diplomat when he was elected pope. He did much to strengthen the supremacy of the papacy in both the East and West and with his *Tome* expounded the doctrine of the Incarnation, accepted at the Council of Chalcedon in 449. He treated with Attila, whose Huns had already sacked Milan, to accept tribute instead of attacking Rome but could not stop the vandal army under Genseric from plundering the city and taking captives. He did, however, dissuade them from burning it. Feast: November 10 (formerly April 11), February 18 in the East.

Other **SS Leo** include four other popes: Leo II (d. 683), July 3; Leo III (d. 816), who after what many considered a miraculous recovery from an attack by his predecessor's relatives, who tried to gouge out his eye and cut off his tongue, returned to Rome under Charlemagne's protection and in 800 crowned him 'Emperor of the Romans' thus allying Church and State in the West, June 12; Leo IV (d. 855), July 17; and Leo IX (1002-1054) a successful military commander as a young deacon but who was captured when leading an army against Norman invaders of Italy in 1052. He travelled widely holding reforming synods, April 19.

Leo Karaasumaru (d. 1597) Korean martyred in Japan. February 6. *See* Francis of Nagasaki.

Leonard (6th century?) A hermit, he founded the monastery at Noblac (now Saint-Léonard near Limoges) where he had his cell. Legend says his prayers saved the life of King Clovis's wife in childbirth, who in thanksgiving gave Leonard as much land as he could ride round on a donkey in one day. Clovis was also said to have promised to free all the prisoners Leonard had visited. Patron of women in labour and of prisoners-of-war. Feast: November 6.

Also another 6th-century hermit who settled near Le Mans. October 15.

Longinus (1st century) The name (probably from the Greek word for lance – *longke*) given to the centurion who thust his spear into Christ's side at the crucifixion. Legend says he was blinded, regained his sight, became a Christian and was later martyred. Some of the First Crusaders claimed to have discovered his lance in a church at Antioch. Feast: March 15.

Louis (Louis IX) (1214-1270) A French king who led the Seventh Crusade and died of plague at Tunis on the Eighth. Patron of Paris. August 25.

Lucian (d. 312) A Syrian priest in Antioch, he founded a theological

53

The Martyrdom and Last Communion of St Lucy *by Paolo Veronese (c.1528-1588).*

school (at which Arian was a pupil) and was an erudite scholar, making versions of the Old and New Testaments used by Jerome in preparing the Vulgate. Died by the sword after torture on the rack during Diocletian's persecution. Feast: January 7, October 15 in the East.

Lucy (d. 304) A virgin martyr who died at Syracuse under Diocletian's persecution. One legend tells how, refusing to marry and denounced by the unwelcome suitor, she pulled out her eyes and sent them to him because he had admired them. They were, however, miraculously restored. Another version says that her eyes and teeth were pulled out at her martyrdom. When flames did not burn her, she was put to the sword. Feast: December 13.

Ludmila (c.860-921) A Slav princess, she was the Christian grandmother of Wenceslaus (q.v.). Her son's widow, fearing she would put Wenceslaus on the throne and reinstate Christianity in Bohemia, had her strangled. Feast: September 16.

Luke (1st century) Author of the Gospel and the *Acts of the Apostles*, he was probably a Greek physician from Antioch who accompanied St Paul on missionary journeys. For a time leader of the Christians at Philippi, he was in Rome on the occasions of both Paul's imprisonments and after his death went probably to Greece where he is said either to have died in Boetia, aged 84, or to have been crucified with St Andrew at Patras. Traditionally, he is said to have painted an icon of the Virgin Mary who appeared to him in a vision though he may have met her in the flesh. Patron of artists, doctors and surgeons. Feast: October 18.

Lupus (383-478) Having been released from a six-year marriage with the approval of his wife, he became a monk, giving his wealth away to the poor. Sent to Britain with Germain (q.v.) and as bishop of Troyes, he bargained with Atilla the Hun to spare his province, offering himself as a hostage. After Attilla's defeat, he was accused of helping him escape and was forced to leave Troyes, spending two years as a mountain hermit before returning to his See. Feast: July 29.

M

Macarius (d. c.830) Called the Wonder Worker, he became abbot of Pelekete where he was imprisoned, tortured and eventually exiled to Aphusia, off the coast of Bythinia, for his opposition to iconoclasm. As his name suggests, he is said to have performed many miracles.
Feast: April 1.

Other **SS Macarius** include two bishops (both 4th century) one of Jerusalem who was with Helena when she found the True Cross and supervised the building of the basilica of the Holy Sepulchre, March 10; a bishop of Petra who resisted theArians, June 20; and two Egyptian hermit monks (again 4th century) who were at one time exiled together on an island in the Nile. Both founders of monasteries, the elder was considered to be a great teacher, January 15. St Jerome adopted some of the monastic rules written by the younger, January 2.

Magnus (d.1116) Son of a Norse ruler of Orkney and a pirate before his conversion to Christianity, he was captured by Magnus Barefoot of Norway and coerced into joining them on their raids. At Anglesey, however, he refused to fight, preferring instead to read his psalter. He escaped to Scotland, living as a penitent until his cousin Haakon gained power in Orkney when he returned to be co-ruler. When he was being murdered by Haakon, he offered himself as a sacrifice and prayed for his murderers.
Feast: April 16.

Malachy (1095-1148) Born in Armagh, where he became monk and abbot as well as abbot at Bangor, he then became bishop of Connor and archbishop of Armagh, though there was conflict over this appointment with members of the family who had long held the post. It was resolved only after his resignation and the appointment of a candidate both parties would support. Malachy returned to the Connor diocese, though dividing it, and himself become bishop of Down. On a trip to Rome he met Bernard of Clairvaux and was eager to join him as one of his monks. The pope insisted he remain a bishop but he founded a Cistercian abbey at Mellifont on his return. Active in restoring religious fervour and rigorously maintaining canon law, Malachy is credited with many miracles which include curing the Scots Prince Henry of an illness. However, the *Prophecies of Malachy* which list the attributes of popes from his own time to the 'end of the world' is a later invention, probably designed to bolster the chances of a papal candidate in 1590. Feast: November 3

Malo or Muchatus (d. c.621) Probably Welsh-born, he was a missionary in Brittany in the area where the town of Saint-Malo was later named after him. Making enemies as well as converts, he and his monks were forced to leave his headquarter at Aleth (Saint-Servan), though he was invited to return shortly before his death. One legend says that once, cut off by the

tide, he was miraculously floated to safety on a bed of seaweed. Feast: November 15.

Marcellus (d. 298) A Roman centurion who, at either Tingis (Tangier) in Morocco or León in Spain, announced his Christianity at an Imperial birthday parade, renouncing his military oath and declaring his service in a temporal army to be incompatible with his being a Christian (*see also* Maximilian). He was tried by the praetorian administration and executed. Feast: October 30.

Other **SS Marcellus** include a pope (d. 309), January 16, and other martyrs: a priest from Lyons (d. c.178) who was buried up to his waist in sand and left to die of exposure at Chalon-sur-Saône, August 26; an Egyptian at Oxyrnychus who was beheaded, along with all the Christians of the town, after fire had failed to burn them, August 27; and a judge from Cyprus and bishop of Apamae, Syria (d. c.389), who were captured, while engaged in destroying a pagan temple and burned. August 14.

Margaret (1247-1297) A Tuscan girl who, unhappy after her father's remarriage, eloped to become the mistress of a nobleman. He was murdered, his dog leading her to his body. She regarded this as a judgement, renounced her possessions and offered public penance. She and her son were befriended by two ladies of Cortona and after several years of devout living and excessive self-mortification she became a Franciscan tertiary, nursing the poor at home and later in the hospital of the community she founded. Feast: May 16.

Other **SS Margaret** include an Englishwoman (d. 1192) who made pilgrimages to Jerusalem and to Spain and France before becoming a Cistercian nun, February 3; a servant of Louvain in Flanders (d. c.1225) murdered by thieves who also killed her employers who had sold their inn prior to embarking on a religious life,

September 2; and a princess of Hungary (1242-1270) who refused marriage and lived a holy and austere life as a nun, January 26.

Margaret or Marina of Antioch (early 4th century?) Legend has it that her father, a pagan priest, drove her out when she became a Christian. She was minding sheep when Olybrius, the governor, saw her and became infatuated with her. Spurned, he caused her to be tortured and imprisoned. The Devil in the form of a dragon appeared and swallowed her but the cross she held grew bigger and bigger until it split the dragon apart and she was able to walk unharmed from its belly. Some versions of the story describe her leading the dragon through the town. After further tortures she was beheaded, as too were the many citizens converted by her preaching and the wonders surrounding her. She may have been a genuine martyr in the time of Diocletian and was one of Joan of Arc's 'voices'. Feast: July 20.

Margaret of Scotland (1046-1093) An Anglo-Saxon princess, she took refuge in Scotland after the Norman invasion, marrying King Malcolm III. Founder of Holy Trinity Church, Dunfermline, and several monasteries, she was a devout supporter of the Church and had considerable influence for good on the Scottish court. Patron of Scotland. Feast: November 16.

Maria de la Cabeza *See* Isidore the Farmer.

Mark (d. c.4) One of the Four Evangelists and writer of the Gospel, he was possibly the son of the house where the Last Supper was held. He accompanied Paul and Barnabus to Cyprus and was with Paul and Peter in Rome. His Gospel was possibly based on Peter's teaching and ideas. Tradition says that he became first bishop of Alexandria and was later martyred.

According to legend, his boat was sheltering from a storm in the Venetian lagoon when an angel proclaimed that a great city would arise there in his honour and that he would found a church at Aquileia. Ninth-century Venetians claimed to have found his body in Alexandria and taken it back to Venice. Feast: April 25.

Martha (1st century) The sister of Lazarus and Mary (q.v.) whom Jesus regularly visited in their house in Bethany. She exemplifies the virtues of an industrious domestic life. Legend says that she later went to Provence where she made converts and overpowered a dragon at Tarascon by sprinkling holy water on it before leading it to Arles, where it was killed. Patron of housewives and cooks. Feast: July 29, June 6 in Greece.

Martin (d. 655) The last pope to be venerated as a martyr, he was arrested

for opposing the Emperor in his support of the theory that Christ had no human will and that people and events in the Old Testament have their counterparts in the New. Imprisoned in Constantinople and charged with treason, his life was spared but he was sent into exile where he died of his ill treatment and privations. Feast: November 12.

Martin of Porres (1579-1639) A lay brother, he was the illegitimate son of a Spanish knight and a black woman. He was apprenticed to a barber-surgeon and this was one of his jobs at the Rosary Convent in Lima. He was active in caring for the sick of the whole city, establishing an orphanage and foundling hospital, and distributing food to the poor. He was unusual, not only for the care he gave to the slaves, but for his love of animals and concern for even rats and mice. Impressed not only by his work and charity but by his devotion, penances and visions, the convent followed his spiritual direction calling him 'father of charity'. He was credited with levitation and bilocation. Patron of social justice and race relations. Feast: November 5.

Martin of Tours (c.316-397) Born in what is now Hungary and the son of a veteran officer, he was enlisted at the age of 15 very much against his will, for he was already attracted to the religious life. One hard winter's night in Amiens, he met a beggar freezing in the cold. He took off his cloak, cut it in two and gave half to the man. That night he had a dream of Christ sleeping wrapped in the portion he had given away. He decided to become baptized and sought release from the army in order to become a monk. Refused his request and charged with cowardice, he offered to go to battle unarmed, but was thrown into prison, then released when the enemy sued for armistice. He became a disciple of St Hilary at Poitiers, then returned to Hungary for a time, making conversions there. He later went to Milan until, driven out

58

by an Arian bishop, he went to live as a recluse on an island in the Gulf of Genoa. In time, he returned to Poitiers, becoming a hermit at Ligugé where a monastic community developed around him, the first in Gaul. The people and clergy of Tours wanted him as their bishop but legend says he avoided this by hiding, only to be betrayed by a cackling goose. A maker of converts, opposer of heresies, destroyer of pagan temples and sacred trees, he was also said to have cured lepers and even raised a man from the dead; he was said to have been tempted himself by devils in the forms of lovely women. When not carrying

out episcopal duties, he lived as a monk at nearby Marmoutier where a great monastery developed, another of the many he founded. Patron of tailors, because of his cloak, he is also the saint of drinkers because, when offered wine by the emperor, he passed it to a poor priest. St Martin's Summer is the name given to the spell of fine weather which sometimes occurs around his feast day. He is also one of the patron saints of France. Feast: November 11, November 12 in East.

Mary (1st century) Sister of Martha and Lazarus (q.v.).

Also Mary the mother of James

the Less who went with Mary Magdalene (q.v.) to Christ's sepulchre and discovered it empty, April 9; and the mother of Mark, whose house was a meeting place for Christ's disciples, June 29.

As the name of Christ's mother (see Mary, The Blessed Virgin) and of other women associated with him, the name Mary has always been a popular name for Christian women.

Other **SS Mary** include a 4th-century slave and martyr, November 1; a Spanish prioress (d. 1290) who aided Christian slaves of the Moors in Barcelona and is patron of Spanish sailors (September 19); Mary Francis

Gallo (1715-1791) a Neapolitan Franciscan nun who received the stigmata, October 6; and Mary Soledad (1826-1887), Mother Superior of the Handmaids of Mary Serving the Sick in Madrid, October 11.

Mary, The Blessed Virgin (1st century) Mother of Jesus Christ. According to the apochryphal *Book of James*, she was born in Jerusalem, the child of Joachim and Anne. Betrothed to Joseph, a carpenter, she was visited by the angel Gabriel who told her that she would bear a child conceived 'of the Holy Spirit'. Joseph, discovering her to be pregnant, also had an angel visitation to reassure him and they were married. The child was born and they went to Bethlehem to register at a census. The bible tells us little about Mary except that she was present at the Marriage at Cana, when water was turned into wine, at the Crucifixion and when the disciples received the gift of tongues at Pentecost. Christ's charge to John at the Cross to treat her as his own mother suggests that thereafter she lived in his household. Later Church doctrine was to develop that she was born without original sin and she was entitled The Immaculate Conception. The concept was hotly disputed between the Franciscans who supported it and the Dominicans who opposed it, as did Thomas Aquinas and Bernard of Clairvaux. Though the doctrine of Mary's Immaculate Conception was celebrated by a feast day from 1476 it did not become defined dogma until 1854. At her death, her body as well as her soul was thought to have been carried straight to heaven. This concept of her 'Assumption' is already evident in apochryphal texts and commonly accepted but was not formulated as dogma until 1950. As the Mother of God she is considered to have a special place in heaven and considerable influence with her Son. Apparitions of the Virgin Mary have led to her veneration at many places associated with the appearances, e.g. Our Lady of

Lourdes, and there are separate feast days to celebrate other events in her life. The first rosary, the string of beads used when reciting prayers to her, was said to have been presented by her to St Dominic in a vision. She is accorded a higher level of veneration than other saints. As The Immaculate Conception she is patron of the United States of America. Other feast days are as follows:- January 1, The Motherhood of Our Lady; February 2, The Purification (also known as the Presentation of Christ in the Temple or Candlemas); February 11, Our Lady of Lourdes; March 25, The Annunciation; May 31, The Visit to Elizabeth (q.v.); July 16, Our Lady of

Mount Carmel; August 15, The Assumption; August 22, The Queenship of Our Lady; September 8, Our Lady's Birthday; September 15, Our Lady of Sorrows; September 24, Our Lady of Ransom; October 7, The Feast of the Holy Rosary; November 21, The Presentation; and December 8, The Feast of the Immaculate Conception, etc.

Mary of Egypt (4th-5th century) A former singer and actress, she engaged in penance for past sins living as a hermit in the Jordanian desert. Another version says she was a prostitute from Alexandria who joined a group of pilgrims to Jerusalem, consorting with

sailors to pay her way and using the journey, perhaps, as a way of getting customers. At the Church of the Holy Sepulchre she felt a mysterious force barring her entry and seeing an icon of the Virgin, to whom she vowed her repentance, she was answered with the message that she should cross the Jordan and would there find peace. Taking only three loaves with her, she went into the desert and lived on dates and berries and when her clothes wore out her long hair clothed her. Thus she was discovered by a monk called Zosimus who heard her story and gave her Holy Communion. Returning he discovered her body and buried her, a lion coming to help him dig the grave. Feast: April 2.

Mary Magdalene (1st century) She was a woman from Magdala, in Galilee, from whom Jesus was said to have driven out seven devils. Later, she was present at the Crucifixion, assisted in the anointing of His body afterwards and was the first to see the resurrected Christ. She may have accompanied John and the Virgin Mary to Ephesus and died there. Western tradition identifies her as the same person who, according to the passage in Luke's Gospel, washed Jesus' feet with her tears, dried them with her hair and anointed them with precious oils, a woman usually interpreted as being a prostitute. She is also identified with Mary, the sister of Martha (q.v.), who traditionally went with her to Provence, hence the many churches devoted to her in France. Modern scholars can find no biblical evidence for considering these to be one and the same person and in the Eastern Church they have always been celebrated separately. Patron of repentant sinners. Feast: July 22, in the East May 4.

Matthew (1st century) Apostle and evangelist (called Levi by Mark and Luke in their Gospels), he was a publican, Galilean tax-collector and author of the Gospel. Tradition holds that after a period of ministry to the Hebrews he travelled to Ethiopia, Persia or Macedonia and that he was martyred, possibly at Myrna by a cannibal king whose subects he had converted. A Talmudic text, however, says he was executed by order of the Sanhedrin. Feast: September 21, in the East November 16.

Matthias Murumba (d. 1887) Martyr. June 3. *See* Charles Lwanga.

Maurice (d. c.287) The commander of the Christian Theban Legion, this Roman soldier raised in Egypt fought the Gauls at what is now Saint-Maurice-en-Valais, near Lake Geneva, where he and his companions refused to sacrifice to pagan gods. Legend says that one in ten were

executed, then, when they still refused, one in ten of those and so on until all 600 (6600 or 6666 according to other versions) were dead. At Vériolez, there is said to be the stone on which he knelt for execution. Patron of Austria, Piedmont, Savoy, Sardinia, and soldiers (especially of the Vatican's Swiss Guard). Feast: September 22.

Mawes or Maudez (5th century?) A monk (or possibly two different monks) from Wales or Ireland, he was a missionary in Brittany and Cornwall and is said to have settled with disciples on the Île Modez off the Brittany coast. He is claimed to be founder patron of the town of St Mawes in Cornwall. Feast: November 18.

Maxentius (c.445–515) His return to the monastery at Agde, in Gaul, which he had entered as a boy coincided with the end of a drought and was regarded as miraculous by the monks. Later, as abbot at Poitou, he was thought to have miraculously prevented soldiers from attacking the monastery. After an austere and holy life he spent

his last years as a hermit nearby. Feast: June 26.

Maximilian (274-295) Son of a veteran soldier and therefore committed to service in the Roman army, he refused the call because he considered that being a soldier was incompatible with his Christian faith.

Beheaded at Theveste (Tebessa), in modern Algeria. Feast: March 12.

Meletius (d. 381) An Armenian, he was elected archbishop of Antioch in 361 and was caught up in the conflict for and against Arianism. Exiled and replaced in his episcopacy, his efforts to regain it were supported by St Basil

although he came into conflict with St Athanasius. He was eventually reinstated in 378. Feast: February 12.

Mellitus of Canterbury (d. 624) Abbot of a monastery in Rome, he was sent with missionaries to help Augustine (q.v.) in Britain in 601. He became first bishop of London but was expelled when the Christian king Saebert was succeeded by pagan sons, traditionally because he refused to give these unbaptized princes Holy Communion. With others from Kent, where the Church was also meeting opposition, he fled to Gaul and was never able to return to London, although he became archbishop of Canterbury in 619. Bede claimed that he saved a church in Canterbury from fire by praying in the path of the flames. Feast: April 24.

Methodius (d. 847) A Sicilian who, after adopting the religious life, built a monastery on the island of Kios from

LEFT
The Calling of St Matthew *by Hendrick Terbrugghen (1587-1629).*

BELOW
Saint Maurice *(detail) by Mathis Grunewald (c.1470/80-1528).*

61

whence he was summoned to Constantinople by Patriarch Nicephorus. When this opponent of iconoclasm was exiled by the eastern emperor, Methodius went to Rome, returning on the succession of a new emperor with an ill-received message from the pope that Nicephorus should be reinstated. Methodius was thrown into prison for seven years, until released by another new emperor, Theophilus. He remained out of favour until on Theophilus' death in 842 his widow, Theodora, repealed the decrees forbidding holy images. Removing the iconoclast patriarch, she installed Methodius in his place and called a synod endorsing the use of icons. Feast: June 14.

Methodius Feast: February 14. *See* Cyril and Methodius.

Michael, The Archangel Leader of the Hosts of Heaven against Lucifer when he revolted against God, and against the dragon described in *Revelations*. It is also said that he will be the Weigher of Souls at the Last Judgement when he will lead the blessed into heaven. Feast: September 29 (now celebrated with Gabriel, Raphael and all angels). Apparitions of the Archangel on Monte Gargano and Mont Saint-Michel are celebrated on May 8 and October 16 respectively.

Milburga (d. 715) A Mercian princess, she was founder of a Wenlock nunnery in Shropshire and its second abbess. She is said to have had powers of healing and levitation. Sister of SS Mildred and Mildgytha. Feast: February 23.

Mildred (d. c.700) Daughter of a Mercian king who entered a convent near Paris to avoid an unwelcome suitor. After receiving education there, she returned to Britain to become a nun at Minster in Kent at an abbey founded by her mother Ermenburga (q.v.). Sister of SS Milburga and Mildgytha. Feast: July 13.

62

Milgytha (d. c.676) Sister of SS Mildred and Milburga. She was a nun in Northumbria, or, according to other sources, in Thanet, Kent, where she succeeded Mildred as abbess. Feast: January 17.

Miltiades or Melchiades (d. 314) He was probably an African and, three years into his papacy, saw the victory of Constantine (q.v.) over Maxentius and the granting of religious freedom in 313. Feast: December 10.

Monica (c.331-387) Mother of Augustine, she was a Christian, probably from Tagaste in modern Algeria and married an ill-tempered and dissipated pagan (or possibly a convert who did not live up to his faith) called Patricius whom she reformed and converted, along with his mother in 370, a year before he died. Neither her own exemplary life nor her arguments managed to turn her eldest son Augustine (q.v.) into a good Christian: he lived a life of dissipation and had a mistress who bore him a son. Turning to prayer rather than confrontation she still sought his reform and, when after studying in Carthage he went to Italy, she followed him to Rome in 383 and then to Milan, living with him and his son. There, she gained the respect of bishop Ambrose (q.v.) who became her son's mentor. After Augustine's reform and baptism in 387, she set out to return to Africa but died at Ostia while waiting to embark. Patroness of wives. Feast: August 27

Mungo or Kentigern (d. 612) Patron of Glasgow, legend says that he was the illegitimate son of a British princess who, when it was found that she was pregnant, was thrown over a cliff and, surviving, was set adrift in a coracle on the Firth of Forth. Reaching shore at Culcross she was sheltered by St Serf and gave birth to Kentigern, named Mungo – 'dear one' – by Serf who reared him. He became a monk at Glasgow, where he

converted the local people before becoming bishop of Strathclyde. For a time, local wars drove him into exile in Northumberland, or possibly even Wales where tradition says he founded a huge monastery at Llanelwy, becoming bishop of St Asaph's. The arms of Glasgow city bear a salmon and a ring, reminder of a legend that he saved the reputation of his queen by restoring to her a ring given to her by her husband, which she, in turn, had given to her lover and which had been lost at sea. It was found by one of his monks inside the fish that had swallowed it. Feast: January 13.

N

Nazarius (1st century) Legend says he was the son of an officer in the Roman army and had heard the teachings of St Peter. During one of Nero's persecutions he was beheaded for preaching Christianity, along with a companion called Celsus. St Ambrose is said to have discovered their bodies in Milan in 395 when Nazarius' blood was said to be still liquid in his veins. Feast: July 28.

Neot (9th century) A monk at Glastonbury, he became a hermit in Cornwall at the place later named after him. King Alfred is said to have gone there to seek his advice. Most of his relics were transferred to a monastery in Cambridgeshire at Eynesbury which was renamed after him. Feast: July 31.

Nicephorus (758-828) A scholarly opponent of iconoclasm, his father, secretary to the Emperor Constantine, had been tortured and imprisoned for his resistance to the abolishment of icons. He became a statesman and an imperial commissioner himself and in 806 was appointed – against his will – Patriarch of Constantinople. In a return to iconoclasm under Emperor Leo, in 813, he was deposed and retired to a monastery on the Black Sea which he had himself founded while still a layman. Despite appeals from Rome for his reinstatement, brought by

Methodius (q.v.), he remained there until his death. Feast: March 13.

Also a martyred priest (d. 260) of Antioch. February 9.

Nicholas (d. c.350) The original Santa Claus, he was a bishop of Myra (Bari) in Asia Minor who was imprisoned during the Diocletian persecutions, opposed Arianism at the Council of Nicea in 325 and was known for his extreme holiness. Legend says that at his birth he stood and praised God and observed Fridays and other fast days by refusing his mother's milk. Feast: December 6.

Nicholas (d. 867) A Roman who held various Church posts, he was adviser to Benedict III before being elected pope in 858. He encouraged missionary work and concern for the poor, supported freedom to marry within Church rules, irrespective of family consent, was firmly against divorce and emphasized papal supremacy over secular rulers in all

matters concerning the Church. Feast: November 13.

Other **SS Nicholas** include a Greek pilgrim (1075-1094) who carried a cross through southern Italy chanting the *Kyrie*, June 2; an Italian friar (1245-1305) famed for his preaching ministry and reported miracles at Tolentino, September 10; a Swiss soldier and magistrate from Flueli who, with the agreement of his wife and family, in 1467 became a hermit, taking only Holy Communion for sustenance. He was consulted by many on account of his wisdom and advised that Fribourg and Soleure be included in the Swiss Confederation, September 25; and a Jesuit martyr, surnamed Owen (d. 1606), an expert in devising hiding places for recusant priests and planning escapes of captives, who was twice caught and tortured, the second time to death, October 25.

Nicodemus (1st century) A Pharisee and member of the Jewish Sanhedrin who sought out Jesus to question him, defended him after his arrest and helped to take Him down from the Cross bringing myrrh and aloes to embalm Him. Legend describes him as a blacksmith because he was thought to have removed the nails from the Cross. Feast: August 1.

Ninian (5th century) Traditionally the son of a northern British chief who went to Rome for his education and returned as a bishop missionary to the north and Scotland, founding a monastery known as the White House, probably at Whithorn in Scotland. He is said to have performed miracles, including giving a blind man back his sight. Feast: September 16.

Noel Chabanel (1613-1649) Jesuit martyr. Feast: October 19. *See* Isaac Jogues.

O

Odo (879-942) Son of a knight and raised in noble households, including that of William of Aquitaine, and founder of the abbey at Cluny, he

64

became a scholar and teacher before becoming a monk at Baume and then the second abbot of Cluny. Insisting on strict observance of the Benedictine rule, he established the abbey's independence from secular authorities and widely extended its influence. Often summoned as a mediator, he acted as peacemaker between Alberic of Rome and Hugh of Provence when he besieged the city.

Other **SS Odo** include a bishop of Beauvais (801-880) who was a soldier before becoming a Benedictine, January 28; an archbishop of Canterbury (d. 959) who encouraged monasticism and scholarship and was later credited with miracles, July 4; and a learned teacher (1050-1113) at Tournai who became bishop of Cambrai but was driven out because he refused to be invested by Emperor Henry V, June 19.

Olaf (995-1030) After a misspent youth raiding in the Baltic and soldiering in Normandy, he was converted at Rouen and recruited to help Ethelred of England fight the Danes before returning to Norway and fighting his way to the crown. He brought peace, law and Christianity, but enforced it harshly. He fled to Russia, returned in an attempt to get back his throne and was killed in battle. Patron of Norway.

Feast: July 29.

Also a martyred King of Sweden (d. 1024), a Christian convert murdered by rebels who were coercing him to sacrifice to pagan gods. July 30.

Oliver Plunket (1629-1681) Member of an Irish royalist family, he spent the years of the English Civil War and Commonwealth studying and teaching in Rome. Appointed archbishop of Armagh and Primate of All Ireland, he returned in 1670, re-establishing the orderly practice of Catholicism in his diocese until persecution led to his going into hiding, then his arrest on charges of conspiracy to organize a rebellion against the crown, involving an army of 20,000 soldiers from France. He was hung, drawn and quartered at Tyburn in London. Feast: July 1.

Omer or Audomarus (7th century) A French monk, he became bishop of Thérouanne in 637 and founded a monastery at Sithiu (now Saint-Omer). Feast: September 9.

Osmund (d. 1099) This Norman noble came to England and became chaplain to William the Conqueror, then chancellor and, in 1078, bishop of Salisbury. He completed the building of the cathedral at Old Sarum, establishing a choir school and a library. A learned man, he was himself a skilled copier and book-binder. He continued to play a role in the administration of the country and contributed to the making of the Domesday Book, which was presented to the king at Old Sarum. Feast: December 4.

Oswald (605-642) Converted to Christianity on Iona while taking refuge in Scotland after his father was killed, he returned south and, after raising a large wooden cross and gathering his small and largely pagan army around it, prayed for victory. That night he had a vison of St Columba casting a protective cloak over his soldiers and next day they killed the British king Cadwallon and defeated his much larger forces. Now King of Northumberland, he sent to Iona for a bishop to convert his land. The first who came was replaced by St Aidan (q.v.) to whom he gave the island of Lindisfarne. Eight years later, Oswald was killed in battle against Penda of Mercia. His last moments were in prayer for the soldiers around him. His body was cut up as a sacrificial offering to Penda's gods. Feast: August 9.

Oswald (d. 992) Born of Danish stock and a nephew of Odo of Canterbury

(q.v.) he became a priest at Winchester, then a monk at Fleury in France. Back in England he was made bishop of Worcester and later archbishop of York, too. Such plurality by a churchman otherwise noted for his reforms was explained by the loss of York lands and Oswald's political involvement with the crown. He founded an abbey at Westbury-on-Trym and was founder-abbot of a larger one at Ramsey (in what was once Huntingdon, far outside his dioceses), where he spent much of his time. It was there that he died during Lent, reciting psalms after performing the daily ritual of washing the feet of paupers. Feast: February 28.

Osyth (d. c.700) A Mercian princess who wished to become a nun but was married to Sighere, king of the East Saxons. Their son, Offa, also once celebrated as a saint (although he seems to have had no official cult), was briefly king but abdicated to go to Rome and become a monk. Despite motherhood, Osyth is celebrated as a virgin. Her legend says that every time her husband tried to consummate their marriage a white stag appeared, either intimidating Sighere or encouraging him to rush off to hunt it. In his absence she sought the protection of certain bishops who persuaded the king to allow her to become a nun and to give her land to found an abbey at Chich in Essex, where she became abbess. She was beheaded by pirate raiders, either resisting them or refusing to sacrifice to their gods after capture, and her body is said to walk, carrying her severed head, to the church where she was buried. Feast: October 7.

P

Palladius (5th century) Possibly a Romano-Gaul sent as a missionary to Ireland as its first bishop, he founded churches there but failed to make many converts transferring his missionary work to Scotland instead. Feast: July 7.

Pamphilus (d. 309) A Phoenician priest from Beirut, he founded a school at Caesarea and built up a considerable library. He was tortured, imprisoned for two years, then beheaded for refusing to make pagan sacrifices. Feast: June 1.

Pancras (early 4th century) This 14-year-old orphan from Phrygia came to Rome with his uncle. There, both were converted and then martyred during Diocletian's persecution. A church dedicated to this saint gives its name to a district of London. Feast: May 12.

Also a martyr (d. c.90) from Antioch, first bishop of Taormina, who was said to have been baptized by St Peter and sent by him as a missionary to Sicily where he was stoned to death by bandits. April 3.

Pantaleon (d. c.305) This physician from Nicomedia, doctor to Emperor Galerius, lapsed but returned to the Faith at the time of the Diocletian persecution, giving away his possessions and tending the poor. He was denounced and beheaded after fire, drowning, attack by wild beasts and other methods failed to kill him. Feast: July 27.

Patricia (7th-century) A noblewoman of Constantinople, she fled to Rome to escape marriage, consecrating herself to God. She returned to Constantinople to give her possessions to the poor, then to Naples, where a phial of her blood is said to liquefy from time to time, like that of St Januarius (q.v.). A patron of Naples. Feast: August 25.

Patrick (c.389-461) A Romano-Briton, he was captured by pirates when young and spent six years as a slave, tending sheep in Ireland. He was promised his freedom in a dream and either escaped or was released. After crossing the country, he begged passage on a ship which, it is said, took him to a strange and uninhabited land from

whence he eventually returned to his family. He studied for the church in Britain and France and, after becoming a bishop, was sent to evangelize Ireland, whose language he now knew. He founded the See of Armagh as the centre for his mission and established a school there. One tradition claims he died at Saul on Strangford Lough, Downpatrick, where he is said to have built his first church. His autobiography and other writings survive. Legend says he expelled snakes from Ireland, used the shamrock to explain the Trinity and converted the country almost single-handed. Patron of Ireland. Feast: March 17.

Paul (1st century) A Jewish tentmaker born Saul, he was a Roman citizen of Tarsus, a strict Pharisee and anti-Christian and was among the people

who stoned Stephen (q.v.). Converted by a blinding vision on the road to Damascus, after which his sight was restored, he was baptized by Ananias, later changing his name to Paul. He meditated for three years in the Arabian desert and returned to preach the Gospel as forcefully as he had previously opposed the Christians, who at first could not believe this *volte face*. Although circumcised himself, he considered this unnecessary for non-Jews contrary to the opinion of St Peter and the Jerusalem Church. However, his view was eventually adopted, thus removing an obstacle to the conversion of gentiles. His missionary journeys to Cyprus, Greece and Ephesus are recounted in the *Acts of the Apostles* including his imprisonment and miraculous release at Philippi – an earthquake broke down the doors of the gaol. In Jerusalem, attacked by Jews who wished to be rid of him, he was arrested, partly for his own safety. Claiming his rights as a Roman citizen, Paul demanded to be tried in Rome for any misdemenour. On the voyage he was wrecked on Malta, eventually reaching Rome via Alexandria. He remained there for two years under house arrest, still preaching and making more conversions. The narrative of the *Acts* goes no further but it is presumed that he was acquitted, for other sources report his presence in Spain and return to Greece and Ephesus. Tradition holds that he either returned to Rome or was taken there and beheaded during Nero's persecution. Called the Apostle of the Gentiles, his feast day, with St Peter is June 29. His conversion is celebrated separately on January 25.

Paul (d. c.345) This Egyptian youth hid from the persecution of Decius and then fled to the desert and lived as a hermit. St Jerome discovered him in old age, the perfect exemplar of a holy man. He is aid to have died aged 113. Feast: January 15.

Other **SS Paul** include a martyr (d. 308) who was beheaded at Gaza, July 25; a Cypriot martyr (d. c.760),

burned for opposition to iconoclasm, March 17; a hermit (d. 956) on Mount Latros and later on Samos, December 15; two Patriarchs of Constantinople, Paul I (d. c.350) who was deposed, reinstated, exiled and eventually strangled, June 7, and Paul IV (d. 784) who sought the restoration of icons, August 28; also, the first pope of that name, another opponent of iconoclasm, June 28.

Paul Miki (1562-1597) Japanese Jesuit martyr. Feast: February 6. *See* Francis of Nagasaki.

Paul of the Cross (1694-1775) Founder of the order of Barefooted Clerks of the Holy Cross and Passion (Passionists). An Italian, he was only 15 when he assumed a life of austerity and mortification, refusing both inherited wealth and marriage, although in 1714 he briefly became a soldier against the Turks. In 1720, a vision of the Virgin Mary instructed him to found his Order, which eventually received papal approval and Paul and his younger brother John, who assisted him, were both ordained. He was a celebrated preacher, said to have gifts of healing and prophecy. Feast: October 19.

Paula (374-404) A Roman mother of five children, she devoted herself to charity after the death of her husband and worked with St Jerome (q.v.). Distressed by a further death, that of her eldest daughter, she made a pilgrimage to the Holy Land, accompanied by Jerome and another daughter, Eustochium, and settled in Bethlehem where they built a monastery and a convent. Her proficiency in Greek enabled her to help Jerome in his studies and she spent her remaining wealth on church-building. Patron of widows. Feast: January 26.

Pelagia (5th century) Legend describes her as an actress – beautiful, rich and immoral – who, on hearing bishop Nonnius of Edessa preaching,

was encouraged to seek baptism. She gave all her wealth to the poor and, dressed as a man, became a hermit. Feast: October 8. (She is also known as Margaret).

Other **SS Pelagia** include a 15-year old martyr in Antioch (d. c.311) who, after being arrested as a Christian, threw herself from a rooftop to preserve her viginity, June 9; and a legendary martyr from Tarsus (d. c.304) who was roasted alive when she refused to become the Emperor's paramour. May 4.

Pelagius or Pelayo (c.912-25) This Spanish boy was given as hostage to the Moors and was tortured to death when he refused to convert to Islam. Feast: June 26.

Peregrine (d. c.261) Was a bishop sent as a missionary to Gaul where he was tortured and beheaded. Feast: May 16.

Perpetua (d. 203) Carthaginian who was arrested in the reign of Septimus Severus. Having survived imprisonment and exposure to wild beasts in the arena, she, Saint Felicitas and others were put to the sword. Feast: March 7.

Peter (1st century) Originally called Simon, he was the brother of Andrew (q.v.), and a fisherman of Galilee on whom Jesus bestowed the name Cephas (Peter, meaning a rock) saying: 'Thou art Peter and upon this rock I will build my Church'. This is when the concept of the papacy was born and thereafter, Peter was recognized as the first pope. He was a married man who left his wife to follow Jesus but took her on some of his missionary journeys. He was present at many of the most important moments of Christ's ministry, including the Agony in the Garden of Gethsemane and Jesus' arrest. However, when asked by the high priest whether he knew Him he denied Him thrice as Jesus had prophesied. After the Ascension, Peter

became the leader of the apostles having had a vision that he should take the Gospel to Gentiles as well as Jews. He baptized Cornelius and was the first to perform miracles. He was imprisoned in Jerusalem by Herod Agrippa but escaped with angelic aid. Non-biblical sources say that he spent many years preaching in Rome and was imprisoned there (and again released by an angel) before being finally martyred, crucified upside-down at his own request so that he would be lower than his Master. Feast: June 29 (with St Paul).

There are many other **SS Peter**, taking their name from the Apostle. Among those not given individual entries are a Palestinian martyr (4th century), January 3; a martyred bishop of Braga (4th century), in Portugal, April 26; a Franciscan (1546-1597) martyred in Japan, February 6 (q.v. Francis of Nagasaki); a missionary and first abbot of St Augustine's Canterbury (d. 606), drowned on a mission to Gaul, January 6; the first hermit on Mount Athos (8th century), June 12; a hermit (10th century) who was a former Doge and commander of the Venetian fleet, January 10; and a hermit (1210-1296), Peter di Morone, who became pope as Celestine V, an unworldly man quite unable to understand the secular role of the papacy and the only pope to have resigned his office, May 19 (dropped in the 1969 reform).

Peter the Martyr (1205-1252) Born in Verona of Cathar parents, he nevertheless became a Dominican friar and a popular preacher. Acquittal of a charge that he had kept women in his cell only increased his fame. Appointed Inquisitor of Milan and northern Italy, he was brutal when suppressing followers of his parents' heresy, which led to his assassination by a Cathar. As he died he prayed for his killer and dipping a finger in his blood traced on the ground the words *Credo in Deum* 'I believe in God'. Feast: April 29.

Peter Nolasco (1182-1256) French-born founder of the Spanish Order of Our Lady of Ransom which ransomed Christian slaves from the Moors. Feast: January 28.

Peter of Alcántara (1499-1562) A Spanish Franciscan who, after being a successful preacher, devoted himself to a life of austerity and prayer, sleeping only one-and-a-half hours a day, eating only once every three days and often fasting much longer. Feast: October 22.

Petroc (6th century) This Welsh monk founded monasteries in Cornwall, including one at what is now called Padstow (meaning 'Petroc's place') and became a hermit on Bodmin Moor. He is said to have performed miracles and had a way with animals – on one occasion sheltering a stag from huntsmen. He made a pilgrimage to Jerusalem and proceeded as far as the Indian Ocean where he established a hermitage on an island there before returning to Cornwall. Feast: June 4.

Philemon (1st century) A convert of St Paul who wrote him an epistle, sending back his slave Onesimus to

him. Tradition says he freed Onesimus and was later stoned to death, together with his wife Apphia, for being Christian. Feast: November 22.

Philibert (c.608-c.685) French monk at Rebais where he was made abbot but resigned because he was unable to exercise proper authority. Later, he founded a monastery at Jumièges, but was imprisoned and forced to leave after opposing the actions of a royal official. He went on, however, to set up other monasteries. Feast: August 20.

Philip (1st century) A fisherman from the region of Lake Galilee, he was already a follower of John the Baptist when called by Jesus to be one of His disciples. In the Scriptures we hear of him on the occasions of the Miracle of the Fishes and the Last Supper. He possibly spoke some Greek, since Greeks approached him to obtain an audience for them with Jesus. Tradition says that he went on to preach in Greece and that he was martyred during the Domitian persecution at Hieropolis, tied upside down to a cross. Feast: May 3, November 14 in the East.

Philip the Deacon (1st century) One of seven people chosen to assist the apostles in Jerusalem, he went on

to preach in Samaria, effecting cures and casting out demons. He was responsible for the conversion of Simon Magus and baptized the first Ethiopian, a eunuch holding high office under Queen Candace. Years later, St Paul stayed in the house in Caesarea where he lived with his four unmarried daughters. Feast: June 6.

Philip Neri (1515-1595) Founder of the Congregation of the Oratory, this Florentine orphan, after some kind of mystical experience, rejected a career with his uncle in return for a life of poverty, tutoring his landlord's sons in lieu of rent before spending several years studying theology and philosophy. Later, he devoted his time evangelizing among the young, encouraging them to devout observances and to the service of needy pilgrims. From these beginnings, he and his confessor brought together a group of laymen from which developed both the Santa Trinita dei Pelligrini Hospital (which later also undertook the care of the sick and the Congregation (or Oratorians), founded in 1564 when Neri, by now a priest and famous as

preacher and confessor, became rector of San Giovanni. In the next decade, the Congregation received papal approval and he was appointed their superior and given Santa Maria in Vallicella which was rebuilt as the Chiesa Nuova and is still its headquarters. Feast: May 26.

Phocas (4th century or earlier) A hermit gardener, he spent his time growing food to feed pilgrims and the poor. However, he was exposed as a Christian and when soldiers arrived, sent to execute him and asking for Phocas he gave them hospitality promising to show them where to find Phocas in the morning. Overnight, he dug a grave, then identified himself, telling the men he welcomed martyrdom and instructing them to behead him. Patron of Black Sea sailors. Feast: September 22.

   Also a bishop from the same place, Sinope on the Black Sea, martyred in the reign of Trajan, July 24; and a martyred bishop of Antioch, March 5. Historically, they may all have been one and the same person.

Phoebe (1st century) Deaconess at Corinth who gave assistance to St Paul. Feast: September 3.

Pius V (1504-1572) Antonio Michele Ghislieri was successively friar, bishop, inquisitor, cardinal and Inquisitor General before becoming pope in 1566 when he was responsible for strenuously enforcing the decrees of the Council of Trent, fighting Protestantism and excommunicating Elizabeth I of England. In the East, he encouraged combined resistance against the Turks and was rewarded by their defeat at the Battle of Lepanto. A former teacher of theology, he led a life of personal sanctity and austerity in contrast to that of many Renaissance popes. Feast: April 30 (formerly May 5).

   Also Pope Pius I (d. c.154), who may have been a freed slave, July 11; and Pius X (1835-1914), August 21.

Pol or Paulinus (6th century) Also known as Paul or Pol de Léon. A Welsh chief's son, he became a hermit at 16, was ordained, and with a small group of followers, became an itinerant evangelist first in Cornwall and then in Britanny where he founded monasteries and became bishop of Léon. Feast: March 12.

Polycarp (c.69-c.155) A disciple of the apostle John and bishop of Smyrna, he was a defender of orthodoxy against Gnosticism and a major figure among Christians of his time. He visited Rome to see Pope Anicetus and fix a date for the celebration of Easter, but they could not agree, thereby establishing two traditions. A second-century account of his martyrdom appears to draw on eyewitness accounts: at the time of persecutions under Marcus Aurelius, following the death of a young man at a pagan festival, the crowd called for action against the Christians and for the arrest of the elderly Polycarp. He

refused to sacrifice to pagan gods, acknowledge the Emperor's divinity or deny Christ answering, 'I have served Him for 86 years and He has never done me ill. How can I blaspheme against my King and Saviour?' The crowd first called for him to be thrown to wild beasts in the amphitheatre, then for him to be burned, but the flames simply billowed around him. He was stabbed to death with a sword or spear. Feast: February 23.

Pulcheria (399-453) A princess of Constantinople, she became regent to her younger brother Theodosius in 414, taking a vow of virginity. She had a sobering influence on the court which had repercussions throughout the empire and was a supporter of papal orthodoxy against Nestorianism. Religious differences and court intrigue after her brother's marriage led to her banishment but she was

recalled and became Empress after her brother's death. She married an elderly general called Marcian, on condition that the marriage was not consummated, and they ruled jointly. She founded churches and hospitals and backed the building of a university in Constantinople. Feast: September 10.

Q

Quentin (3rd century) He was beheaded at Augusta Veromanduorum, now known as Saint-Quentin, in Gaul. According to legend, he was a Roman who preached in Amiens and was first arrested and imprisoned there, forced to endure red-hot nails driven into his head and shoulders and impalement on a pit before execution. His body was thrown into the Somme with a millstone tied around the neck. Fifty years later it is said to have floated to the surface uncorrupted. Feast: October 31.

R

Radegund (518-587) The father of this Thuringian princess was murdered and she herself was taken as a captive by the Franks. When she was only 12, she became a Christian and at 18 married King Clotaire. For six years, she devoted herself to the poor and sick while he mocked her childlessness and consorted with other women. When he murdered her brother she left him and became a nun at Saix, later founding a monastery at Poitiers which she developed as a centre of learning. Christ is said to have appeared to her in a vision, leaving his footprint on the paving of her cell, now preserved in her church at Poitiers. Feast: August 13.

Ralph or Raoul (d. 866) Son of a French count, he became abbot of several monasteries, founder of others and bishop of Bourges, being renowned for his great learning. Feast: June 24.

Raphael, The Archangel. Acknowledged by Jews, Christians and

Moslems, although he is not named in the canonical books of the Bible, he features in the apochryphal Book of Tobit where he appears to Tobias disguised as a young man Azarias. Feast: September 29.

Raymond of Peñafort (1175-1275) Preached the Spanish crusade that freed Spain from the Moors and is considered to be co-founder of the Mercedarians with St Peter Nolasco (q.v.). Feast: January 7.

Among other **SS Raymond** are two more Spaniards: the founder and abbot of Fitero (d. 1163) who raised an army and formed the Order of the Knights of Calatrava to fight the Moors, February 6; a member of the Order of Our Lady of Ransom (c.1204-1240), who remained as a hostage in Algeria when the money he used to ransom Christian slaves ran out. He was tortured when it was discovered that he had attempted to convert Moslems, and was made a cardinal on his return to Spain. Known as Nonnatus ('not born'), his mother died before he could be born and he was removed from her womb after her death. He is patron of midwives and of Catalonia, August 31.

Remi or Remigius (c.437-533) A Gaul of noble birth, he was already famous as a youth for his preaching. He was made bishop of Rheims, crowning King Clovis, whom he converted. After the recovery from sickness of the king's young son and a victory over the Alemanni were attributed to Christ in answer to the prayers of Queen Clotild, who was already a Christian, Remi went on to baptize the rest of the king's family and followers and spent his life evangelizing among the Franks. It was claimed that holy coronation oil was brought to him by a dove and that he had a special power, which he passed on to Clovis – the ability to cure scrofula (the King's Evil) by touch. The same power was later claimed by

Edward the Confessor (q.v.). Feast: October 1 (January 13 in Rheims).

René Goupil (1606-1642) Jesuit martyr. Feast: October 19. *See* Isaac Jogues.

Rita of Cascia (1377-1447) Married for 18 years from the age of 12, despite her wish to enter a convent, to an unfaithful husband who treated her badly, she gained her freedom when he was murdered as a result of a vendetta. When her sons also died she attempted to enter a convent but was refused because she was not a virgin. Finally, however, she became a nun at the convent of Santa Maria Maddalena at Cascia in 1413. The remainder of her life was spent in austerity, full of penance, prayer and meditation on Christ's Passion. After listening to a sermon on the Crown of Thorns, she developed a forehead wound, as if made by a crown of thorns, which would not heal and which she bore until her death 15 years later of tuberculosis. Like St Jude, she is a patron of hopeless causes. Feast: May 22.

Robert (1027-1110) Born of nobility in the Champagne area of France and a monk at 15, he was soon a prior, an abbot and then abbot of a new community at Molesme. In 1098 some of the monks began to find that the rule had become lax and they transferred to Cîteau to live by the stricter Benedictine Rule with Robert as their abbot. Later, the Pope ordered him back to Molesme. Feast: April 29.

Also three English **SS Robert**: a hermit (1160-1218) who lived much of his life in a cave at Knaresborough, September 24; a Cistercian abbot (c.1100-1159) who was one of the founders of Fountains Abbey and then abbot at Newminster in Northumberland, June 7: and a boy (1171-1181) at Bury St Edmunds whose death was blamed on Jews. Never an official saint, this was probably an example of medieval anti-Semitism as with Hugh of Lincoln.

Roch (c.1293-c.1327) In order to help the sick and poor, he gave away a wealthy inheritance and became a pilgrim, spending three years in Rome. Finding himself in a plague-ravaged city, he stayed to nurse the sick and at Piacenza developed plague himself. Here he might well have died had a dog not brought food to him. When he eventually returned to his home town of Montpellier he was unrecognizable because of his emaciation and was thrown into prison as an imposter. Only when he died five years later was his identity confirmed by a birthmark. Some say that he was imprisoned in Lombardy as a suspected spy and credit him with miraculous cures as well as tending plague victims; others say a dog licked his sores and cured them and an angel comforted him in prison. Invoked against pestilence. Feast: August 16.

Roderic (d. 857) A Spanish priest, he was denounced by his brother, a Moslem, who claimed he was an apostate of Islam. He was imprisoned and eventually beheaded. Feast: March 13.

Romulus (1st century) Traditionally a convert of St Peter, he became bishop of Fiesole, Italy, and was martyred during the Domitian persecution. Feast: July 6.

Rose of Lima (1586-1617) A Peruvian, she was the first saint of the New World to be canonized. Born in Lima of Spanish parents who had lost their wealth, she supported her parents by needlework and floristry. Refusing marriage and taking a vow of virginity, she became a Dominican tertiary, living in a garden shed and mortifying herself with penances that included wearing a crown of thorns and sleeping on broken glass. A church commission examined her after she claimed visions and mystical experiences and decided they were genuine. Her prayers are credited with saving Lima from an earthquake. Patron of South America and the Philippines. Feast: August 23.

Rose of Viterbo (1234-1252) Having experienced a vision of the Blessed Virgin at the age of 8, she began to preach four years later, calling on the people to support the pope and defy the Emperor Frederick II who had invaded the papal states and taken Viterbo. The emperor's supporters sought her death but she was banished instead, returning after Frederick's death (which she had prophesied). The local convent refused to take her as a nun because she had no dowry and when the local priest set up a house and chapel for her and her followers, so that they could live a religious life, the nuns insisted it be closed. She was therefore forced to return to her parents where she died aged only 17. Feast: September 4.

Rufina (d. c.287) Martyr, sister of Justina (q.v.). Feast: July 19.

Rufus (d. c.107) Originally from Antioch or Philippi, he arrived in Rome with St Ignatius of Antioch (q.v.) and was thrown to wild beasts in the colosseum during the reign of Trajan. Feast: December 18.

Rumwald (7th century) Legend says that as this Mercian prince lay dying, aged only three days, he said, 'I am a Christian', demanded baptism and Communion, sermonized with quotations from the Scriptures and the Creed and gave instructions that he should be successively buried in three places – King's Sutton, Brackley and Buckingham. Feast: November 3.

Rupert (d. c.710) A Frank or an Irish bishop of Worms and Salzburg, he was a missionary along the Danube and in Bavaria and founder of a monastery at Salzburg (where he also developed salt mines) and a convent at Nonnberg. Feast: March 27.

S

Sabina (d. c.120) Legend says that she was a wealthy Roman widow who died for her Christian faith in the reign of Hadrian. Feast: August 29.

Salome (1st century) Mother of the apostles James (q.v.) and John (q.v.), wife of Zebedee and one of the women who discovered Jesus' empty tomb. Feast: October 22.

Sava (1173-1236) A Serbian prince, he became a monk on Mount Athos with his father, who abdicated his throne. He founded Khilandari monastery, returned to Serbia to complete the conversion of the country and founded other churches and monasteries, mediating in civil wars between his brothers and becoming archbishop of Zica. He made a pilgrimage to Jerusalem, where he built the monastery of St John and was on a second journey there when he died. He made or commissioned translations and wrote monastic rules and other works important to the development of Serbian literature. Feast: January 14.

Scholastica (d. 543) Sister of St Benedict (q.v.), she was founder of a convent at Plombariola, near Monte Cassino, and was considered to be the first Benedictine nun. Benedict had a vision of her soul flying to heaven as a dove and was thus forewarned of her death. Brother and sister were buried in the same grave at Monte Cassino. Feast: February 10.

Sebastian (d. c.290) A Gaul from Narbonne, he became a member of the Praetorian guard and a favourite of the Emperor Diocletian. A secret Christian until two of his friends were tortured, he declared his own faith, making many converts in the process, and was sentenced to be executed by archers. Riddled with arrows and left for dead, he was rescued and nursed by St Irene (not the Macedonian saint), widow of the Emperor's chamberlain, St Castalus, who was smothered in a pit for helping Christians. Diocletian discovered Sebastian had survived and ordered that he be clubbed to death. Patron of archers, athletes and soldiers. Feast: January 20.

Sergius (1315-1392) Son of a Rostov noble family which fled Tartar invasion to become peasant farmers at Radonezh, near Moscow. Here, after the death of their parents, both he and his brother became hermits and founded or restored the Holy Trinity monastery, Sergius becoming abbot. His influence was considerable and he was invited to be Metropolitan of Moscow, but refused. Many attributed the Muscovite victory over the Tartars in 1380 to the power of his prayers. Feast: September 25.

Silas or Silvanus (1st century) A leading Christian of Jerusalem, he accompanied Paul on some of his journeys and was imprisoned with him at Philippi. Traditionally, he is held to be first bishop of Corinth and to have died in Macedonia. Feast: July 13.

Silvester (d. 335) He became pope at the beginning of 314, soon after the empire introduced religious tolerance and Christianity was recognized. Constantine gave him the Lateran Palace, but stories of him baptizing the Emperor and receiving the Donation of Constantine (which gave considerable temporal power to the papacy) in return for curing him of leprosy, are inventions. Constantine was baptized on his death bed after Silvester's death, and the Donation was a much later forgery. Feast: December 31, January 2 in the East.

Simeon or Simon (1st century) A devout Jewish priest, it was ordained that he would see the Messiah before he died and he met the Holy Family when the baby Jesus was presented in

OPPOSITE
St Roch *by Carlo Crivelli (1430/5-c.1495).*

BELOW
St Irene Removing Arrows from St Sebastian's Leg *by Georges de La Tour (1593-1652).*

the Temple in Jerusalem. Holding Him in his arms, he was inspired to speak the words of the *Nunc dimittis*. Feast: October 8.

Simon (1st century) One of the apostles, he was known as 'the Zealot' either for his strict adherence to Mosaic law or for his support of opposition to the Roman presence in Palestine. One tradition describes him as a missionary in Egypt and Mesopotamia with St Jude (q.v.), both being martyred in Persia. Feast: October 28.

Simon Stock (d. 1265) An English friar, he appears to have undertaken a pilgrimage to the Holy Land and become a Carmelite hermit, returning to England to Aylesford when the Saracens drove them out. In 1254, he became Superior General of the order in London, at the end of a period when it was evolving into an order of mendicant friars. He established many new houses in the British Isles, France and Italy. He is said to have had a vision in which the Virgin Mary promised that anyone who died wearing the Carmelite brown scapular would be saved. Feast: May 16.

Simon or Simeon Stylites (c.390–459) The first and most famous of the pillar hermits, he was first a monk, practising extreme mortification which included the wearing of a belt of twisted palm leaves which so cut into his flesh that it took three days of softening them with oils before they could be removed. Appalled, his abbot dismissed him, but he became a hermit and decided to fast for Lent. A priest set out loaves and water for him but at Easter he was found unconcious, the food untouched. After three years, he removed himself to a mountain top near Antioch, where he chained himself to a rock. But he attracted crowds of the curious and sick wishing to touch him in the hope of a cure. In 423, therefore, he set up a pillar 9 feet (2.75 metres) high, made from three slabs of stone to represent the Trinity,

so that he could perch on it and escape their attentions. This was replaced by successively higher pillars so that for the last 20 years of his life he was 60 feet (18.5 metres) in the air on a platform only 6 feet (1.8 metres) wide. Here, he prayed and preached to the faithful and sightseers (including three emperors), while others consulted him by letter. Feast: January 5, September 1 in the East.

He had his imitators, including Daniel (q.v.) and Simon Stylites the Younger (6th century) of Antioch who lived on a pillar for 68 years, starting at the age of 7. September 3.

Sixtus II (d. 258) Possibly a Greek philospher, he became pope a year before being arrested for preaching or conducting mass in a cemetery outside Rome. His deacon Laurence (q.v.) was arrested soon after. Feast: August 6.

Also Pope Sixtus I (d. c.127), who may also have been martyred, April 3; and Sixtus III (d. 440), August 19.

Sophia Despite the supposed dedication of the great church, now a

TOP
The Stoning of St Stephen *by a Spanish follower of Luca Giordano, c.1720.*

ABOVE
St Stanislaus *by an unknown Gothic Hungarian artist, c.1490.*

mosque, in Istanbul, Sophia is not a saint, merely the Greek word for 'wisdom' and *Aghia Sophia* is in fact the Church of Holy Wisdom, *Sancta Sophia* in Latin, thus leading to the persistent misunderstanding. However, in order to explain the Christian principles of Faith, Hope and Charity, they are allegorized as the martyred daughters of Wisdom who dies mourning them. All August 1.

Spiridion (4th century) A Cypriot shepherd, he was made bishop of Tremithus because, though uneducated, he was famous for his knowledge of the Bible. Punished for his Christian faith during the persecution of Galerius Maximian, he had an eye gouged out and a hamstrung cut before being sent to work down the mines. Feast: December 14.

Stanislaus (1010-1079) This Polish priest became a famous preacher and bishop of Cracow. He threatened cruel King Boleslaus with excommunication if he did not change his ways and, after his attempted abduction of a nobleman's wife, anathematized him. Boleslaus found him celebrating Mass in St Michael's chapel outside the city and killed Stanislaus himself. Patron of Cracow. Feast: April 11.

Stanislaus Kostka (1550-1568) This Polish youth was educated at the Jesuit College in Vienna. He was eager to join the Society of Jesus but either the Viennese Provincial refused to accept him or his father objected, so he walked barefoot to Rome where Francis Borgia admitted him to the Society aged 17. He died only nine months later during which time he practised mortification and saw visions. Feast: November 13.

Stephen (d. c.35) A Jew, he became one of the first deacons appointed to adminster the early Church in Jerusalem. He was accused of blasphemy and answered the charge with a long sermon-like defence. But his accusers, who included St Paul (q.v.), were unconvinced and dragged him out of the city and stoned him to death, thus making him the first Christian martyr. Feast: December 26.

Other **SS Stephen** are a pope (d. 257), August 2; the first king of Hungary (975-1038) and responsible for establishing Christianity, August 16; a Saxon missionary bishop (d. c.1075) martyred in Sweden, June 2; the English-born co-founder of the Cistercian Order (surnamed Harding (d. 1134) who became third abbot at Cîteaux, July 16; and a French hermit (1047-1124) who wore a metal breastplate next to his skin and founded the Order of Grandmont, February 8.

Sulpicius (d. 647) As bishop of Bourges he defended the rights of the people against the king. Feast: January 17.

Swithin or Swithun (d. 862) A royal chaplain and adviser to the king of Wessex, he was bishop of Winchester from 852 and noted for his simple life and efficient administration. He asked to be buried outside in the churchyard but his body was later transferred to a shrine in the cathedral in 971, when it rained for 40 days. This is the origin of the tradition that if it rains on July 15 (his feast day) it will continue to rain for the next 40 days.

T

Teresa of Avila (1515-1582) Spanish mystic and famous founder of the reformed or Discalced Carmelites. As children, she and her brother set off to find Moors in the hope of being martyred and going straight to heaven. Their uncle stopped them and took them home where they began to build themselves a hermitage in their garden. After her mother's death, when she was 15, Teresa was sent to a convent to be educated but fell ill and was nursed at home. Eventually, she persuaded her father to allow her to become a nun, although she was still often ill. She was much influenced by Augustine's (q.v.) *Confessions* and identified with him and Mary Magdalene (q.v.). She began to have visions and hear voices which troubled her until her confessor convinced her that they originated from God. Her health was restored in middle age, and in 1562 she founded the Convent of St Joseph, which had a more severe régime than the Calced Carmelites, and later sixteen others together with a monastery for men. By this time she had met St John of the Cross (q.v.) and with him went on to establish more foundations, though both met considerable opposition from the more relaxed Carmelites. She wrote a celebrated autobiography and several spiritual works. Patron of Spain. Feast: October 15.

Teresa of Lisieux (1873-1897) Known as 'The Little Flower', she was the youngest daughter of a watchmaker, brought up by sisters and aunts after her mother's death when she was 5 years old. She longed to follow her elder sisters and become a nun but was regarded as still too young. However, she was allowed to enter the Carmel convent at Lisieux in the spring of 1888. In 1895 she suffered a haemorrhage, symptomatic of the tuberculosis which proved fatal and prevented her from going out to Cambodia as a missionary as she had planned. Before she died, she wrote the story of her childhood and continued it to cover her life in the convent. It was later published as *The Story of a Soul* and is still famous worldwide. Co-patron of missions and of France. Feast: October 1.

Theobald (d. 1066) The son of a French count who, together with his friend Walter, rejected their lives as knights to become hermits, working as farm labourers and masons to earn their keep and building themselves cells at Rheims, then in the Ardennes, in Luxembourg and finally, after a pilgrimages to Santiago de Compostela and Rome, in Salanigo, near Vicenza, Italy. Walter died two years later and Theobald became a priest and joined the Camaldolese Order. Feast: June 30.

Theodora (d. 310) Legend tells how she was the wife of a prefect of Egypt who, in penance for a sin, left him and entered a monastery disguised as a man, her sex being undiscovered until her death. Feast: September 11.

Also another Egyptian (d. c.304) who was sentenced in the Diocletian persecution to work in an Alexandrian brothel for refusing to make pagan sacrifices. She was rescued by a man called Didymus but immediately died. Didymus was later beheaded. Both April 28.

Theodore (d. 613) Son of a Galatian prostitute, who ran an inn, and a circus acrobat, he was devout even as a small child, missing mealtimes to attend church. Meanwhile, the arrival of a superb cook so improved his mother's business that she gave up prostitution. Theodore lived for a time in the cellar of his mother's house, then in a cave under a chapel and finally, seeking even greater austerity, in a walled-up cave on a mountain. After a pilgrimage to Jerusalem, he became a monk and took to living in a wooden cage, then in an iron one, hung in the air above his cave. He wore metal bands on his hands and feet as well as an iron collar and belt and a breastplate to increase his discomfort while fasting excessively all the while. Here, he attracted many followers and visitors and a church and monastery developed around the cave. He was unwillingly made bishop of Anastasiopolis which he relinquished after ten years and retired to his monastery at Sykeon whence he was called to Constantinople by the Emperor. Here, as elsewhere, he is said to have performed miracles, including curing the emperor's son, possibly of leprosy. Feast: April 22.

Other **SS Theodore** include a soldier-martyr (4th century) who burned down a pagan temple and was executed in Thrace, November 9; another soldier-martyr of about the same period who was a general and governor of Pontus, February 7; a Greek-born monk (602-690) who became archbishop of Canterbury, founded a school there and held the first synod of the Anglo-Saxon Church, September 19; the reforming Byzantine abbot (759-826) of Studios and other monasteries, whose conflicts with Emperors Constantine and Nicephorus and with Patriarch Nicephorus led to imprisonments and banishments, November 11; and an English martyr (d. 870) killed by Danish raiders. April 9.

Theodosius (d. 1074) An important figure in the development of Russian monasticism, he came from a wealthy family but, having unsuccessfully attempted a pilgrimage to Jerusalem, gave up a comfortable life to do menial work and joined the hermit Antony Pechersky in a cave above the River Dnieper. Around it developed the Monastery of the Caves of Kiev where he eventually became abbot. He somewhat relaxed the austerity of Antony's rule, stressing service to others as well as prayer and study. Feast: May 3.

Thomas (1st century) A Galilean Jew, he is traditionally known as an architect and builder. His name means 'twin' and is used in its Greek form of Didymus in John's Gospel. He is known as the doubting Thomas who insisted on touching Christ's wounds before accepting His resurrection but was the first to acknowledge His divinity. One tradition holds that he took Christianity to Parthia but the existence of an ancient Christian community on the Malabar Coast of India lends some credence to the claim that he converted their ancestors and was martyred and buried at Mylapore, now part of Madras. Another version of the story says he converted a ruler in the Punjab and was accidently killed by an archer who was shooting peacocks. Feast: July 3, October 6 in the East.

Other **SS Thomas**, in addition to those listed separately, include a monk (d. 1295) killed in a French raid on Dover, August 2 (locally only); an Italian shepherd who became a Franciscan (1656-1729), said to have been an ecstatic and to have levitated, January 19; a Spanish Franciscan (1486-1555) who preached at the court of Charles V and became archbishop of Valencia, September 22.

Thomas Aquinas (1226-1274) Born at Aquino, in Italy, and educated at Monte Cassino monastery and Naples university, he became a Dominican against the wishes of his family and a leading theologian, teaching mainly in Paris but also at Naples, Rome, Orvieto, Viterbo and Anagni and writing *Summa Theologia* and other

works. As a young man, his brothers regarded him as over-studious and brought a woman to his room. Thomas snatched a piece of burning wood from the fire, drew a sooty cross on the wall and chased her out. It was said that two angels brought him a symbolic girdle of chastity and thereafter he was never tempted again. Patron of universities and of booksellers. Feast: January 28.

Thomas Becket (1118-1170) A Londoner of Norman stock, he joined the staff of the Archbishop of Canterbury, becoming a legal expert and negotiator. On Canterbury's recommendation, he became Henry II's Lord Chancellor and a close friend of the king with whom he led an army into battle. Henry, expecting thereby to have the Church securely in his pocket,

contrived to have Thomas elected archbishop of Canterbury. But as archbishop he fought for the rights of the Church, continually opposing the king until he was forced to flee into exile to Pontigny in France. A fragile peace was made, however, and Thomas returned to Canterbury in 1170. However, a ceremony to crown the Prince of Wales (a way of ensuring the succession without contest) without his authority led to his excommunicating the Archbishop of York and other bishops and their continued defiance of papal authority reopened old antagonisms. In the presence of courtiers, Henry exclaimed in exasperation 'who will rid me of this troublesome priest?' Seeking to comply with his wishes, several of his knights set off for Canterbury and murdered

LEFT
The Murder of St Thomas Becket, a 13th-century psalter illumination painted twenty to thirty years after his death.

RIGHT
St Thomas More with His Family *by Rowland Lockey (painted c.1593). Thomas is left of centre wearing his chain of office as Lord Chancellor.*

Thomas in front of a side altar in his own cathedral. Henry accepted some responsibility and performed public penance. Thomas' tomb became one of the most important shrines in Christendom and a pilgrimage centre to compete with Santiago de Compostela and even Rome. Feast: December 29.

Thomas More (1478-1535) Born in London, he was an eminent lawyer, scholar and humanist thinker and the author of *Utopia* which formulated ideas for the perfect commonwealth. A prominent parliamentarian, he also became Speaker of the House. Henry VIII, whom he had taught as a young man, sent him on diplomatic missions

and appointed him Lord Chancellor. More angered the king, however, by refusing to sign a petition to the Pope seeking approval for his divorce from Catherine of Aragon and further opposed measures taken by the crown against the Church. More resigned and withdrew from public life but his reputation was great and Henry felt the need to regain More's support even though the full weight of his censure was as yet unspoken. But More's continued refusal to sign a document repudiating papal authority and supporting the divorce – though he was prepared to accept any future children of Henry and Anne Boleyn as heirs to the throne – led to his imprisonment in the Tower of

London, and his continued silence to his trial and execution on a charge of treason. Feast: June 22.

Timothy (1st century) A convert to Christianity, he was a disciple of St Paul (q.v.), who became his friend and correspondent. Son of a converted Jewess and a Gentile father of Lystra (in modern Turkey) he was circumcized after conversion to please the Jewish Christians. According to tradition, he was the first bishop of Ephesus and was said to have been clubbed and stoned to death at a pagan festival. Feast: January 26, January 22 in the East.

Other **SS Timothy** include an Egyptian martyr (d. c.286) who was

tortured and nailed to a wall together with Maura whom he had recently married, both taking nine days to die, May 3; and a martyred bishop of Gaza (d. 304) who was tortured, then burned, August 19.

Titus (1st century) A convert of St Paul, he later became his secretary. Unlike Timothy (q.v.), with whom he shares a feast, Paul would not allow him be circumcized. First bishop of Crete. Feast: January 26, August 25 in the East.

Trophimus (3rd century) Sent from Rome with St Denis (q.v.) as a missionary to Gaul, he became first bishop of Arles. Feast: December 29.

U

Uncumber or Wilgefortis (date unknown) Legend says that she was one of a septuplet of daughters born to a pagan king of Portugal. She was desperate to avoid a planned marriage to the king of Sicily because she had taken a vow of virginity. In answer to her fervent prayers, she grew a beard and moustache and the groom understandably called off the wedding. As a result, her furious father had her crucified. Thomas More (q.v.) said the name Uncumber had come about because English women, wishing to uncumber themselves of cumbersome husbands, prayed to her, making an offering of oats. Deriding the practice, he hazarded an explanation that the oats was provender for a horse for the husband 'to ride to the devil upon'. It is possible that she never existed, the name Wilgefortis coming from the Latin *virgo fortis*, 'steadfast virgin'. Feast: July 20.

Ursula (4th century) Her romantic story tells how she was the daughter of a Christian king of Brittany betrothed to a British pagan prince who postponed the marriage for three years to allow her to make a pilgrimage to Rome. With ten of her ladies, each accompanied by 1000 attendants, Ursula travelled up the Rhine in a boat piloted by an angel. In Rome they met the prince, who had arrived there by another route, and he was baptized. Returning home, they were captured by Huns besieging the city of Cologne. Ursula, refusing the advances of their leader, was shot with an arrow and the other 10,999 girls were massacred rather than lose their virginity. Another version tells how she sailed from Cornwall to Brittany with even more attendants! The story possibly originated when an inscription was found in Cologne commemorating the restoration of a church in honour of some local martyred virgins. It includes the Roman numerals XI MV which

possibly referred to XI (11) *Virgines Martyres*, but was misread as XI mille (thousand) virgins. Feast: October 21.

V

Valentine (3rd century) The bishop of Terni, he was beheaded in Rome. A crow at his execution was said to have indicated to other Christians where he was buried.

Also a priest and doctor martyred

on the Flaminian Way in the reign of Claudius the Goth and who it was said had given a blind girl back her sight. These two saints may in fact be one and the same person and neither of them is in any way associated with lovers. The idea is more likely to have its origins in a pagan festival held in mid-February when boys drew lots bearing the names of unmarried girls. Feast: February 14.

Vedast or Vaast (d. 539) This French priest was associated with St Remi (q.v.) in missionary work and is said to have prepared King Clovis for baptism. He was later bishop of Arras, where his efforts firmly established Christianity. Feast: February 6.

Veronica (1st century) She is said to have approached Christ as he carried His Cross to Calvary and to have wiped his brow with a cloth on which the image of his face became imprinted. Later, she became a Christian and is said to have given the cloth to Pope Clement. Her name comes from *vera icon*, 'true image', and suggests that her story may have been invented to explain the relic, now in St Peter's in Rome, which has been venerated since at least the 8th century. There is, however, no mention of her in earlier accounts. Feast: July 12.

Victor (d. c.287) A soldier who refused to accept the belongings of dead members of the Christian Theban Legion or to make pagan sacrifice. Martyred with Maurice, (q.v). Feast: October 10.

Other **SS Victor** include a soldier martyred at Marseille after torture (d. 290), July 21; a Moor in the Praetorian Guard (d. 303) martyred in Milan during the Maximian persecution, May 8; an African-born Pope (d. c.199), July 28; a Carthaginian-born bishop of Vita, in Africa (d. c.505), August 23; a learned bishop of Capua (6th century), October 17; and a French hermit (d. c.610) who made many converts in Champagne, February 26.

Vincent (d. 304) Trained for the priesthood by bishop Valerius of Saragossa, he was arrested and imprisoned with him. Valerius was exiled and Vincent was tortured and died in prison, but not before he had converted his gaoler. Feast: January 22.

Other **SS Vincent** include a bishop of Cracow (c.1150-1223) who resigned to become a monk and wrote the first chronicle of the kings of

Poland, March 8; and the son of an Englishman settled in Valencia, called Ferrer (1350-1419), who became a Dominican preacher and tried to persuade the anti-pope Benedict XIII to end the Great Schism, April 5.

Vincent de Paul (1580-1660) A Franciscan, he founded the Congregation of Mission Priests and Sisters of Charity. Son of peasant

RIGHT

St Vincent and a Donor, *by a 15th-century Master of Archbishop Dalmau of Mur.*

BELOW

St Veronica *by Domenikos Theotokopoulos (El Greco) (1541-1614).*

OPPOSITE

St Ursula and the Eleven Thousand Virgins *by Jacopo Robusti (Tintoretto), (1518-1594).*

farmers in Gascony and educated by Franciscans and at Toulouse university, he became a court chaplain and tutor to the family of an aristocrat until a false accusation of theft and the final confession of a dying peasant opened his eyes to the spiritual health of the French peasantry. He managed to combine his ministry to the rich and powerful – which included Margaret of Valois, Louis XIII and Anne of Austria – with his concern for the poor, establishing a perpetual mission. This was carried out by the Mission Priests (often known as the Lazarists after their Paris church) who devoted themselves to smaller towns and villages and the

Sisters of Charity who tended the sick. He was also active in ransoming Christian slaves; there is an unsubstantiated story that he was himself captured by pirates and sold into slavery in Algeria in 1605. Patron of all charitable societies. Feast: September 27.

Vitus (d. c.300) One story tells how he was martyred in Lucania, in southern Italy; another that he was martyred in Sicily with two others, Modestus and Crescentia. Legend says that angels danced for them in prison and that, after torture, they were thrown to a lion, which simply licked

their feet. So they were put into a cauldron of boiling oil and a wolf watched over their bodies until they could be given a proper burial. Vitus is patron of epileptics, sufferers from snake bite, from chorea (St Vitus' Dance), and of dancers and actors. Feast: June 15.

Vladimir (955-1015) The Russian Prince of Novgorod, he fled to Scandinavia when his half-brother captured the city but later consolidated a cruel and barbaric rule over Russia which stretched from Kiev down to the Crimea. Conversion came with his marriage to a daughter of Emperor

Basil II when he reformed his life, lavishly bestowing alms and establishing many churches and schools. Feast: July 15.

W

Walburga or Walpurgis (d. 779) She was the daughter of an Anglo-Saxon chief, becoming a nun at Wimborne in Dorset, and was sent to help her uncle St Boniface's missionary work in Germany where she became abbess of Heidenheim (which had been established by her sister Winnibald as a combined monastery for monks and nuns). She studied medicine and a curative oil is said to flow from the rock on which her reliquary rested. Walpurgisnacht, the day of her translation to her shrine at Eichstatt in Bavaria, coincides with a pagan witch festival but its occult traditions have no connection with the saint. Feast: February 25.

Wenceslaus or Vaclav (907-929)

A Bohemian ruler, he was raised a Christian by his grandmother and succeeded as king when still a boy. His mother was appointed regent and favoured anti-Christian elements, but despite opposition, Wenceslaus set about the complete Christianization of his land. When he married and had a son, his brother Boleslav saw his own chances of succeeding disappearing and threw in his lot with rebels who resented the influence of the clergy. Boleslav, inviting Wenceslaus to celebrate the feast of SS Cosmas and Damian with him, killed him as they arrived at the church door. As he died, Wenceslaus asked God's forgiveness for his brother. The familiar English Christmas carol dates from the 19th century and draws on an incident mentioned in one 10th-century text but is not included in other lives of the saint. Patron of Bohemia.
Feast: 28 September.

Wilfrid (c.634-709)

Educated at Lindisfarne, Canterbury and Rome, he became a monk in Lyon under the Roman, rather than the Celtic rite. Back in England as abbot of Ripon, he began to introduce Roman ways, arguing the case for their way of calculating Easter, and ensuring that it was adopted. He was then appointed bishop of York but returned to France for his consecration, discovering on his return that Chad had taken his place. For a time he was reinstated but disputes with the Crown and Canterbury continued. Wilfrid was imprisoned for a time and then expelled to southern England, where he continued his missionary work.
Feast: October 12.

William (d. 1201) Said to have been a fisherman from Perth, in Scotland, he devoted himself to the care of paupers and orphans and set off for Jerusalem with one companion, his adopted son, who murdered him near Rochester for his possessions. A woman who found his body was cured of her madness and other miracles were claimed. Feast: May 23.

Other **SS William** include a duke of Aquitaine (d. 812) who became a Benedictine monk, May 28; an abbot at Dijon (962-1031) who made St Benignus into a major monastic centre, January 1; an Anglo-Saxon (d. 1070), chaplain to King Canute, who went with him to Denmark and, shocked by the irreligious state of the country decided to stay there to improve it, becoming bishop of Roskilde in Zeeland, September 2; a French canon at Tours (d. 1090) who studied medicine, went soldiering, then became a hermit and went to Jerusalem, April 24; an Italian hermit (1085-1142) who founded a strict monastery, moving on to found others when its members found its rule too austere, June 25; an English archbishop of York (d. 1154), deposed, restored, and some say poisoned, June 8; a loose-living French soldier (d. 1157) who reformed and went on a pilgrimage to Rome and then to Jerusalem and became a hermit, February 10; a bishop of Saint-Brieuc (d. 1234), July 29; a Dominican (d. 1242), sent to counter the Albigensian heresy in Languedoc who was murdered when a guest of the Count of Toulouse; and an English boy (d. 1144) found dead in a wood near Norwich. At a time of anti-semitism, Jews were unjustly accused of torturing and crucifying him (q.v. Hugh), March 24.

Winifred or Gwenfrewi (7th century) Legend says that Prince Caradoc attempted to seduce her with a promise of marriage and, when she refused, chased her and cut off her head. A spring or fountain flowed from the spot where her head struck the ground at what is now Holywell, in Clwyd. Her uncle, the abbot Beuno, also celebrated as a saint, reunited head and body and brought her back to life. She became a nun and later abbess at Gwytherin. Feast: November 3.

Y

Yves, Ives or Ivo (c.1235-1303) A Breton lawyer and Franciscan tertiary who, even as a student, practised monk-like austerities. In court, he defended widows and orphans free of charge. As a judge in the Church court at Rennes he attempted to persuade litigants to settle out of court. Ordained in 1284, he became a parish priest and built a hospital where he often tended the sick himself, offering his own clothes and bed to beggars. From time to time he acted as an arbitrator although he was no longer a court official. Feast: May 19.

Z

Zacharius or Zachary (1st century) The husband of Elizabeth and father of John the Baptist (q.v.). When he doubted the angel who announced that he and his elderly wife would have a child, he was struck dumb, regaining his speech after the birth when he wrote down the child's name as John. Feast: November 15.

Zeno (d. c.372) Originally from Africa, he was an active opponent of Arianism and the author of many homilies, later becoming bishop of Verona. A keen angler, his fishing was interrupted by a messenger sent to fetch him to exorcize the Emperor's daughter for which his reward was the imperial diadem which he broke up and gave to the poor. The messenger stole a fish but found it would not cook. Patron of Verona.
Feast: April 12.

Zenobius (d. c.390) A member of the important Florentine family Geronimo, whom he later converted, he became a friend of St Ambrose (q.v.), a diplomat at the Vatican and bishop of Florence. It was said that he raised five people from the dead and that when he died his body, which crowds were clamouring to touch, was pushed against a withered tree which promptly burst into leaf. Patron of Florence. Feast: May 25.

Zita or Sitha (1218-1278) All her life she was serving maid to a wealthy family in Lucca. Many miraculous events are connected to her. Angels are said to have made the bread which she neglected to bake in favour of her devotions; a coat belonging to her master, which she gave to a beggar without permission, was returned to him by an angel; loaves she had taken to give to a starving family turned into roses when it was discovered she had purloined them and water given to a pilgrim turned into wine. Patron of Lucca and of domestic servants (invoked particularly for lost keys). Feast: April 27.